Quick and Fun
Games for Toddlers

Grace Jasmine

 Teacher Created Materials, Inc.

Edited by Stephanie Buehler, M.P.W., M.A.

Illustrated by Victoria Ponikvar-Frazier

Cover Design by Chris Macabitas

Made in U.S.A.

ISBN 1-57690-359-1

Order Number TCM 2359

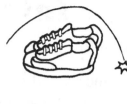

Table Of Contents

Outdoor Games

Indoor Games

Toddler Tips

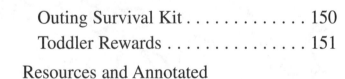

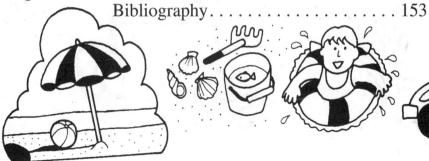

Introduction

Oh, You Must Have Been a Beautiful Baby!

Has there been a time recently when you looked at your beautiful baby and realized that he isn't a baby anymore? Your baby has grown to be that terrific but tiring small child known as a toddler. What exactly is a toddler? A toddler is a child who can move around independently.

And move they do! If you have a toddler, you know that newly independent toddlers are into everything. Toddlers are also known for being in love with the world. They generally have a sunny perspective and are rarely bored because they have so much to learn and do. With your guidance, toddlers have the opportunity to discover many new and exciting things.

So how does a parent channel a toddler's natural curiosity? *Quick and Fun Games for Toddler* is one answer. The indoor and outdoor games in this book are easy to do. They relate to the seasons, months, and holidays, and they will help you bond with your special little one. They are designed to help you create an enriching environment for your toddler that can help him thrive and reach his highest potential. This is especially important during the toddler years. Developmentally, your toddler's brain is programmed to take in all kinds of stimulation from the environment; rich connections are being formed that can influence his later ability to learn.

Why Games?

First of all, games are a fun part of life. Secondly, the games in this book will set the stage for your toddler to . . .

- follow directions
- listen
- work and play with others
- take turns
- gain social skills
- enhance early, oral language skills
- set the stage for reading readiness
- sequence items and events
- increase cognitive thinking skills
- improve large and small motor skills

Most of the games in this book require little or no preparation. Some games make use of things you already have in your home or your toddler's toy box. Others require some simple construction with a little gluing, cutting, and pasting. Occasionally, you will prepare something that you and your toddler will use outdoors later.

A Few Thoughts About Competition

Many—though not all—of the games in this book were conceived as races, with a winner being declared at the outcome. After all, our society values competition; at the same time, we also value good sportsmanship and try to teach children to play for the love of the game. All of this may be quite a lot to convey to a toddler, but you can still lay the groundwork for future competition and sportsmanship by doing the following:

- Make winning a sign of mastery rather than superiority. Praise the winner for having good skill, rather than for being "better" than the other player. Encourage the other player to work on the skill as well.

- Take winning lightly. A simple "Good job!" and a pat on the back will convey the message you wish. And there's no reason why the same message can not be given to all the other players as well.

- Teach sportsmanship by having players cheer for each other and by shaking hands or giving a high five after a match.

- Play some rounds of a game without winners, just for practice. That way you can decide the skill level of the players ahead of time and either give a handicap to the more skilled player or make everyone a winner just for playing.

- Teach the losing player positive self-talk. The losing player can tell herself, "I can win if I practice," "I can have fun even if this isn't my best game," or "I'm still okay whether I win or lose."

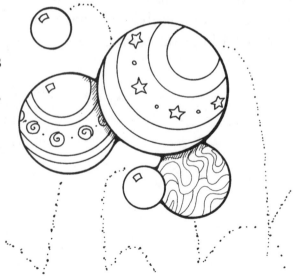

As you read over any games that are described as races, you can certainly decide to modify them so that they are simply activities to enjoy without competition.

Two Ways to Play

This book has been written as two books in one. The outdoor games are seasonal games that relate to months of the year, holidays, or special times that come during those months. The indoor games feature different areas in your apartment or home so that you and your toddler can have fun no matter where you are. Pick and choose the games you wish to play in the way that is most convenient to you.

A Salute to Parents of Toddlers

If you are chasing your toddler through a store while you are trying to read this introduction, you may not realize that this special period will be over before you have had a chance to rest your feet. Cherish this time with your little one and give yourself the extraordinary gift of innocence, laughter, and love. We hope you and your toddler will have many happy hours together playing games from this book.

Tips for Raising Terrific Toddlers

Your Toddler Knows More Than You Think

Many parents believe that their toddler is too little to understand much of anything. This is a misguided notion. While it is easy to think that a small child isn't listening to what you say, toddlers do have a basic sensitivity to those around them. Take care to watch your words and avoid unintentional hurts while you are around your toddler.

It Is the Parents' Job to Help a Child

Toddlers are at the beginning stage of making sense of the world around them. Because of this, parents have a special responsibility to interact with their toddlers, helping them make meaning out of experiences and events. Communication with a pre-verbal child is just as important as communication with an older child. In fact, your ability and willingness to communicate clearly and carefully with your toddler can have a great impact on his or her later mental, emotional, and social development.

Language and Your Toddler

This book is designed for use with toddlers who may be at any number of developmental levels. As you use these games with your toddler, don't be concerned if some seem harder for her than others or don't interest her at all. Make note of the games that are successful, and play them often. Go back later to those games that didn't seem to work with your toddler; notice changes in interest level and development that occur over time.

Toddlers typically gain vocabulary at a rapid rate. As you talk with your toddler, pay attention to the new words and phrases she uses. Even if your toddler is not yet verbal, continue to talk to her. Speak clearly with a warm and animated voice. Keep at it, as you are your child's first and most important language teacher.

Communicating with Your Toddler

The following tips can help you effectively speak with your toddler:

- Toddlers may not be able to understand what you say, but they often can understand your mood or how you feel about something. They may not be able to pinpoint what is wrong in a situation, but they often can tell when you are happy, sad, or angry. If the situation is appropriate (e.g., a friend is moving away and you are sad), label your own feelings for your toddler. This can help him begin to identify and name his own feelings.

- Toddlers need to be spoken to constantly about what you are doing and why. Toddlers generally understand far more language than they can speak. Don't think that just because your toddler isn't very verbal yet that he doesn't have increasing understanding of what he sees and hears around him.

- Toddlers should never be exposed to violence or adult subject matter on television, even if you don't think they can understand what is being said. Young children cannot yet tell what is real and what is fantasy; violent scenes can be very disturbing for a child who can't verbalize his fear.

- Toddlers need to be spoken to in a friendly, loving tone of voice. They need to be reprimanded firmly but kindly. Toddlers don't have the cognitive ability to make connections between cause and effect except on the most fundamental level.

Communicating with Your Toddler *(cont.)*

- Toddlers have differing ability levels. Although many parents worry about their child's development, there is a very broad range of what is considered normal development. If you do have ongoing concerns, consult with your pediatrician, who may refer you to a specialist to assess and treat any obstacles to normal development.

- Toddlers can't be expected to know right from wrong, to share, or to control their tears. Think of them as walking babies who are also just learning the babysteps of behavior.

- Toddlers need to be distracted and/or removed from troublesome situations or environments. While you can talk very simply with your toddler about acceptable and unacceptable behavior, remember that toddlers do not yet have the ability to reason. Don't expect them to generalize from one situation to another and to understand your expectations for their behavior in each one.

- Toddlers also don't have a concept of what it means to be naughty. For the most part, they do not intentionally misbehave. They are experimenting with behavior and testing to see what response it will get. Again, firm but kind correction or distraction are the key to early training.

- Toddlers love attention. There will never be a time that your child will be more loving and cuddly as when he or she is a toddler. Take advantage of the close moments and cuddle time, and make learning about life with your toddler a happy and instructive game.

Safety at Home

Safety First

If you are the parent of a toddler, you know that your child moves quickly and has unpredictable behavior. This is normal. Because your child cannot yet reason, you have the responsibility to monitor and protect your child. What follows are common-sense rules for protecting your toddler in a variety of situations.

At Home

- Never leave your toddler alone or unsupervised.
- Never leave your child around a swimming pool unattended—even for a second. The sound of a child drowning is silence.
- Be sure that you drain wading pools, water tables, and buckets after play.
- Be sure your toddler doesn't sample nature by putting leaves, berries, or other natural items in her mouth.
- Be sure your toddler's shoes are safe, easy to move in, and always fastened.
- Be sure that any boards, nails, or other dangerous building materials are removed from your backyard.
- Be sure your fence and gate are secure.
- Be sure that your toddler's toys are safe and free from small parts.
- Be sure your child's play materials are nontoxic.
- Be sure your child wears sunscreen and a hat when out in the sun.
- Be sure all household pets are toddler-friendly.
- Be sure barbecue items are safely put away.
- Be sure your toddler never plays in a driveway in which an unsuspecting motorist can back out or pull in suddenly.

Safety in Public Places

Safety First, Wherever You Go

Public places are wonderful locations to experience life with a toddler. Use the following tips to make sure you cover the bases to protect your toddler, no matter where you go!

In Public Places

To protect your child in public places . . .

- Never leave your child alone—ever.
- Never ask a stranger to look after your child, even for a second.
- Always watch your child carefully near an ocean, river, or lake. Water currents can easily knock over a small child. Hold your toddler's hand even while dipping toes in the water.
- Be sure that your child is water-safe as early as possible, but be aware there is a great difference between a child who is water-safe and a swimmer.
- Be sure that your child has appropriate tetanus vaccinations.
- Always stand near your toddler when he or she plays on playground equipment.
- Never leave your toddler alone in a car, boat, or any other vehicle.
- Use insect repellent and be sure that your toddler wears socks in heavily wooded or natural areas.
- Watch your toddler for signs of heat exhaustion on especially hot days. Provide a water bottle, boxed juices, or access to a drinking fountain.

Don't Worry—Take Action

While most parents are aware of these tips, it is still a good idea to review these lists when you leave your toddler with any child-care provider or sitter. Consider copying pages 9 and 10 for your refrigerator door.

How to Use This Book

Using this book with your toddler is easy. All you have to do is pick a place to start. There is no right way to use the games in this book; it is up to you and your personal preferences, where you are, and the time of year. If you use the outdoor activities, consider the suggestions in the sections that follow.

Think Seasonally

Winter, spring, summer, fall—you and your toddler will have a ball! This cheerful book is designed to be used in a variety of settings that take advantage of seasonal changes and holidays.

This book is also especially designed to be used outdoors. Some places to play toddler games include the following:

- the backyard
- the front yard
- the sidewalk
- the neighborhood schoolyard (after hours)
- the park
- the beach
- the lake
- the car
- the supermarket
- the train station
- the airport
- waiting in line
- waiting in a restaurant

Take Out Your Calendar

Begin the fun and games by taking out your calendar. Look through the pages of this book, starting with the seasonal section you find yourself in today. Then, read the activities and think about which ones might work best for your toddler. Select a game and scan the "Materials" section at the side of the page. This section lists everything you will need to begin the game. Mark your calendar with the dates you plan to try a game. Sometimes it is also helpful to make a little note of the title of the game you would like to try. You can also keep this book in the car or your backpack for those outings that take you and your toddler beyond the backyard.

How to Use this Book *(cont.)*

Toddler Observation Journal

You may wish to create and maintain your own observation journal. Observation is the process early childhood educators use to learn how children behave over time so as to assess their development.

You can learn this same method quickly and easily for the price of a small notebook and a pen. All you need to do is record your observations about each game that you and your toddler try. Describe what your toddler did, what she seemed to like, what she was good at, what she didn't master, and so on. Then write your own reflections about the game. Keeping an observation journal about your toddler can also be a wonderful keepsake.

Form a Parent-Toddler Buddy Team

Life is more fun with a buddy so consider enlisting one of your friends who also has a toddler to help you experience the games in this book. You then will have support and someone to discuss each game's results with as you go along. You will also have someone to share preparation time, driving, and other responsibilities.

Consider Your Local Resources

As you begin to use this book, think about the resources you have all around you. Consider getting a guide book from your local automobile club about the landmarks that interest tourists when they come to your area. Use this information to make outings interesting for you and your toddler. You will never be in a rut again.

Check out some of these places:

- state parks
- museums
- outdoor exhibits
- annual fairs and other once-a-year local traditions
- public parks
- school grounds you have never been to
- tourist attractions
- libraries
- pick-it-yourself farms and fruit stands

How To Use This Book *(cont.)*

Indoor Fun

What if you feel like staying inside where it may be warmer or cooler than it is outdoors? No problem, just begin with indoor games, starting on page 80. All you need to do is review the selection of games and decide where you and your toddler would like to begin. Notice that in this portion of the book, the games center around common rooms in a house. This is another way to help foster early learning in your toddler.

Maximizing the Experience

To make each game experience a happy one . . .

- Expect your toddler to have difficulty understanding all of your directions.

- Be flexible and willing to play along with your toddler, rather than always insist he do it your way.

- Dress your toddler in play clothes that can get messy and wash easily.

- Use the games in the book any way you want to—from cover-to-cover or at random.

- Remember your toddler has a short attention span.

- Remind yourself that your toddler is just learning about the world around him.

- Read over the games before you try them and prepare materials ahead of time.

- Keep a journal of your play experiences.

- Take a camera along sometimes to capture precious moments.

- Enjoy yourself, too!

Outdoor Games

Seasonal Activities by Month

Pine Cone Pick-up

Materials

- Two large grocery bags
- An area with pine cones on the ground
- Plastic eyes (optional)
- Pompoms (optional)
- Felt (optional)

Pine cones are fascinating things. Children love to pick them up and look at them. Take advantage of this fascination with a natural item by using pine cones for a game.

Set out on your winter walk with a large grocery bag each for you and your toddler. Guide the walk to an area with pine trees or other cone-bearing trees. Call your toddler's attention to the cones on the ground and challenge her to fill her grocery bag before you can fill yours. (Make sure that the area is not environmentally protected and that it is legal to remove the pine cones.) Once you have collected your cones, there are several games you can play:

- **Fill the Bag:** Who can be first to fill a bag? Give a prize to the winner.

- **Pine Cone Count:** Who can gather the most pine cones? Count them. This is a simple game and an excellent way to practice counting.

- **Prettiest Pine Cone:** As a first activity in aesthetics, try to find the prettiest pine cone. Compare and see. What makes a pine cone beautiful? Talk about it with your toddler.

- **Biggest and Smallest:** Look over your bounty to find the biggest and smallest pine cones. Sort the pine cones by size. Line them up in ascending or descending order according to size.

Pine Cone Pick-up *(cont.)*

These are great games to do before a pine cone craft session. A really easy idea is to make pine cone folks by gluing on plastic eyes, pompom noses, and mouths cut from felt.

Snow Babies

Materials

- Lots of snow
- Snow clothes
- Camera (optional)
- Hot cocoa and warm fire (optional)

Making snowmen can be great fun, but snowmen are just too big for your toddler to manage, even when he or she is just helping. This snow game becomes a contest for you and your toddler, and "snowmen" become "snow babies," little figures that you and your toddler will enjoy making.

Begin by showing your toddler how to roll an average snowball. Help your toddler practice making snowballs, working on a few together. Make three snowballs and use them to create a snow baby. Once your toddler gets the idea, have a race to see who is fastest at making a snowball and then a snow baby.

Have your other children involved in this game and make a whole snow family. Try having everyone make a snow baby, then have a snow baby beauty contest, voting to decide the favorite. See who can make the littlest snow baby. Make a number of them and then after you are done, jump on top of them and start again! Take pictures of the snow babies with a camera so that you will have a keepsake long after the snow babies melt. After you have had enough play, run inside for some hot cocoa and a warm snuggle by the fire. Watch the snow outside the window and make up a story about the snow babies and their snow family.

Rain Measuring Game

Materials

- Four plastic tumblers
- Red nail polish

Rain, rain go away, come again another day! Even if the rain won't go away, you and your toddler can still have a wonderful day playing this Rain Measuring Game. Nothing is worse than being trapped inside because of bad weather. Toddlers hate it, and so do their parents. But you can both find some consolation in measuring the rain.

Begin this game by marking off inches on four clear, plastic tumblers with red nail polish. Then mark the tumblers with the initials of both you and your toddler so you will know who wins this contest. Put on your raincoats and go outside with your toddler. Place two of the tumblers out in the open and place the other two under the trees. Which tumbler will fill with rain first? Will each pair fill up equally? Who will be the winner?

Go back inside and read stories or color with crayons, then put your raincoats back on and go check the results. This activity can give you something interesting to look forward to all day. Let the winner choose a video to watch, or make popcorn and read more stories. Soon the rain will end and you will be going on outings again.

Spring Toy Race

Materials

- Two metal or plastic spring toys
- Front porch steps or other outdoor staircase

This game is for toddlers and their parents in parts of the country without snow. All you need are two spring toys and some stairs. You can find spring toys such as Slinky® at any toy store. Spring toy races can be very exciting and are easy for you and your toddler.

Begin by finding a staircase. You can use your front porch steps or travel to a high school and use the steps in the stadium. Just remember to use caution around steps with your child. A good idea is to start at the bottom of a staircase, position your child there, then stretch up and place the spring toys five or six steps up from your position. This way, you and your toddler are not actually on the staircase and can see the race clearly.

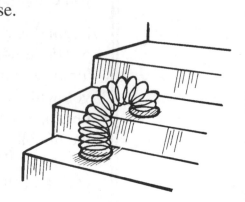

Get the spring toys started by tipping the first metal coil over the top step. Watching the toys will soon have you giggling. Name your spring toys and cheer the winner.

Try a variation by getting a few more spring toys and watching them go all at once. These toys are very inexpensive, so this idea isn't out of the question. Also, check out plastic spring toys if you prefer them to the metal ones.

Pet Races

Materials

- Pets with leashes
- Stuffed animals with string or ribbon

This game is for two toddlers who have pets. Make a play date with another parent, toddler, and their pet. Arrange to go for a walk. The toddlers and their pets can race from tree to tree or from any other landmark you decide upon. You can do this in a park or on your own lawn—it doesn't matter. Don't worry about mismatched pets; whether the racers turn out to be two dogs or a dog and a turtle, it will still be fun for the toddlers. Be aware of animal safety and rules in your particular city. You may choose to hold your animal race at a "pooch park" or other approved location.

For toddlers who don't have pets, try this variation. Get two toddlers together for a race with their favorite stuffed dogs. Tie a length of string or ribbon around each stuffed animal's neck and let the children race their dogs by pulling them along. As odd as this seems, toddlers love this idea and are totally caughtup in the imaginary play. After the stuffed puppies race on the grass, try putting them on the swings to see which puppy you can push the highest. Or try racing the stuffed animals on a slide, placing both puppies side-by-side and letting them speed to the bottom.

Make sure that the stuffed puppies you select are washable. Most stuffed animals will easily survive a nice washing and drying, which they will most likely need after this activity.

Wishing Well Game

Materials

- Washtub or large plastic container
- Pennies
- Golf balls (optional)

If you have ever wished for an easy and interesting game to try with your toddler, the Wishing Well Game might be the answer. By using simple items you almost certainly have on hand, you can be playing instantly. This game will help your toddler develop accuracy at throwing, as well as large and small motor coordination.

Prepare for play by filling a large washtub or other large plastic container with water. (You may want to set up the tub in the bathroom or kitchen to make cleanup easy.) Then dive into your wallet or piggy bank for some pennies. Give your toddler a handful of pennies. Tell him to make wishes and throw the pennies one-by-one into the "wishing well." Count how many times he can hit the water. Get involved and take turns. As your toddler plays, he will develop more accuracy.

If your toddler is at a stage in which he can't be trusted with a small object, use golf balls instead of pennies. Golf balls are easy for a toddler to manipulative and they make a nice little splash when they hit the water. After you are done, let your toddler fish out the pennies or balls. Dipping a hand in the water to retrieve the pennies will be just as much fun for your toddler as throwing the pennies in the first place.

Paper Heart Hunt

Materials

- Red and pink construction paper
- Large sheet of paper
- Nontoxic glue
- Scissors
- Candy conversation hearts (optional)

Celebrate February and Valentine's Day by saying "I love you" to your toddler in a very special way. As with an Easter egg hunt, this game requires your toddler to find paper hearts that you sprinkle around your patio and garden. This game is great for two or more toddlers.

Prepare for this game by cutting out lots of red and pink construction paper hearts in different sizes. Keep in mind that the more hearts your toddler finds, the happier she will be.

Give your toddler a basket to carry for placing the paper hearts in as she finds them. See how fast your toddler can find the hearts, then count how many she has found. Remember to count the hearts before you place them so you will know when she should stop looking—and to avoid frustration, don't make the hiding places too difficult.

After your toddler is finished, give her a candy conversation heart for each paper heart collected. If you don't want to give candy, give a kiss or hug for each heart instead. Then get a large piece of construction or butcher paper and let your toddler glue the collected hearts to the paper. This collage can make a wonderful valentine to give someone, too.

Match the Shoe Relay Race

Materials

- Pairs of shoes
- Outdoor play area

Any game that teaches a child to pick up his shoes has got to be a winner. If you have a collection of your toddler's old shoes, you have everything you need to play. If your toddler doesn't have a lot of old shoes, add the shoes of other family members.

In an outdoor, grassy playing area, line up one of each pair of shoes along the starting line. Deposit the second shoe from each pair in a pile at the other end of the area. Your toddler grabs one shoe at the starting line and then runs to the pile of shoes, rummages through it until he finds the matching shoe, then returns both shoes to the starting line. He grabs another shoe at the starting line and repeats the process until he has found all of the mates for each shoe.

This game can be played with any number of players. While your toddler is having a wonderful time, he will also be learning to match two objects—an important early-childhood learning skill. Finish the game by putting all the shoes neatly away in the closet.

What Am I?

Materials

• None needed

Toddlers love to guess. As they are learning more and more about the world around them, they will want to show what they know with this fun guessing game. Begin this game by using some of the following examples. After you have repeated the clues, let your toddler guess the answer. Make sure to pick things that are familiar to your toddler. Soon your toddler will want to try giving clues, too!

Examples:

I am round.

I have numbers on my face.

You use me to tell the time.

I go tick, tick, tick.

What am I? (Clock.)

I am furry.

I am an animal we have in our house.

I purr.

What am I? (Cat.)

I am an animal.

I bark.

I wag my tail.

What am I? (Dog.)

I am someone who loves _____ very much.
(Toddler's name.)

Who am I?

You can play this game again and again. Try playing it while driving or waiting in line.

Sidewalk Pattern Game

Materials

- Two pieces of sidewalk chalk in different colors
- Outdoor sidewalk

This recognition game is a first step to building mathematical pattern awareness in your toddler. The patterns used in the game are called "A-B patterns." Put simply, this means that only two elements, A and B, are used for making a repeated pattern. Patterns are not only an early math skill but also a logical and critical thinking skill.

Start this game by finding two different colors of sidewalk chalk; an A-B pattern will make more sense to a toddler if each element is a different color as well as a different symbol. Then find a span of sidewalk and draw some A-B patterns. As you draw, tell your toddler you are making a pretty pattern and ask him to help. Try these patterns first:

X O X O X _____

Show your toddler what comes next. Try another:

A B A B A _____

Again, show your toddler what comes next, or see if he can tell you.

You can use any two symbols in an A-B pattern. Try happy faces and stars or anything else your toddler will enjoy. Don't make a pattern more than two elements for this age group. Your toddler wins when he correctly picks the next element in a pattern. Before you know it, your toddler will be challenging you with patterns, too.

Stop and Go Safety Clu~

Materials

- Blank notebook
- Stickers

As soon as your child can walk, you need to educate him about safety around cars. Crossing the street safely will be one of your toddler's big accomplishments as he grows older, and it is never too early to reinforce pedestrian safety.

Begin this game by buying a blank notebook and some colorful stickers that your child likes. Each time you cross a street with your toddler say, "Now, we have to stop, look, and listen." Show your toddler how to do this by modeling it every time you cross the street. In fact, this game is one you can expect to do again and again for years.

After your child has seen you model the "stop, look, and listen" process, you will be ready to make it into a game. At each stoplight or street crossing say, "What should we do here?" When your child gives you the correct response, give your child a sticker for his sticker book. The receipt of tiny rewards will make learning about pedestrian safety fun and motivate your child to practice it.

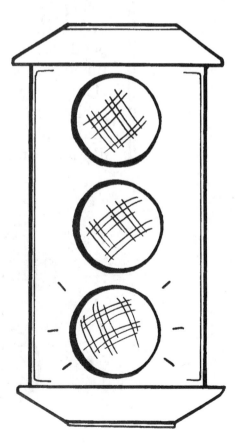

Toddler Triathalon

Materials

- Outdoor play area
- Tricycle or push car
- Ball
- Ribbon for the winner

Do you ever dream about training your toddler for the Olympics? Even if you or your toddler doesn't have any such aspirations, this triathalon game will help her build large motor skills, endurance, and coordination. She also will learn to follow directions and take turns—the beginnings of becoming a good sport.

A triathalon is an athletic competition that has three different events which follow one right after the other. In this game, your toddler will go around a sort of obstacle course three times. Invite siblings and/or friends to participate and add to the excitement.

Begin this game by setting up your child's triathalon event. Decide what events you would like to have. A good idea is to have a tricycle or push-car riding event, a running event, and a ball-bouncing event. Take your child through the course and then let her do it again and again. Make a ribbon for a prize and hang it around her neck. Add drama to the event by pretending your child is a real athlete in a real competition; she will love it!

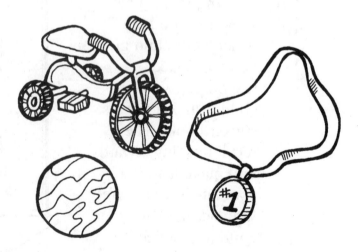

Toddler Twigs

Materials

- Outdoor playing space
- Tricycle or push car
- Ball
- Ribbon for the winner
- Pond or lake
- Two twigs or sticks

You will discover that sometimes the very best games you and your toddler can play are the kinds you make up on the spot, don't have hard-and-fast rules, and don't require any equipment. If you find yourself near a pond or lake with your toddler one afternoon, play a game of "Toddler Twigs."

Begin this game by finding a shallow pond or lake area. With your toddler, pick out two twigs or sticks that are big enough to throw. Then look at the pond together and decide where you will throw the sticks in the water. You can make the "finish line" for the twig anywhere you would like and make the rules as simple or complicated as you wish.

Play variations of this game by gathering a lot of sticks and seeing who can throw a stick the farthest. Try floating a number of sticks, pretend they're boats, and have a boat race! Talk with your toddler about how he wants to play and let him help make the rules.

Morning Workout

Materials

- Comfortable shoes
- Workout or play clothes
- Outdoor playing space

If you are going to keep up with your toddler while he or she grows, you are going to have to stay in shape. This game is an excellent way for you and your toddler to get into the routine of a morning workout. This game uses a traditional children's song with words altered to fit the game. Sing the song and do the actions with your child. Once your toddler has caught on, let her pick the actions to fill in the song each time. You both successfully complete the game by being able to do all of the actions mentioned in the song.

> *This is the way we hop, hop, hop,*
> *Hop, hop, hop,*
> *Hop, hop, hop.*
> *This is the way we hop, hop, hop,*
> *In our morning workout!*
> *(Sung to "So Early in the Morning")*

Use some or all of the following actions to make this musical game a great workout for both of you:

- hop
- skip
- touch your toes
- bend and stretch
- jump
- run in place
- clap your hands
- twirl around

Demonstrate how to do those actions that your toddler can't yet do, and each time you play this workout game you will see an improvement. Add a different action in every line of the song to make it more challenging. See if you can both win by doing every action correctly without missing one.

Catch the Baby

Materials

- Slide in your backyard or park
- Baby doll

"Here comes the baby, sliding down the slide! Can you catch her?" Don't worry, because the "baby" in this game is a doll. When toddlers play with baby dolls, they learn a lot about empathy and kindness. Playing with a pretend baby is an excellent way to learn about how to care for another person.

Begin by finding one of your toddler's dolls to use as the "baby" in this game. Use your backyard slide or take your toddler to her favorite park slide. Position your toddler at the bottom of the slide, instructing her to "Catch the baby!" Take the doll to the top of the slide and send it down with a reminder to your toddler about her task. Try this again and again. Each time your child catches the baby without letting it fall, she has completed the game successfully.

This game gives you the opportunity to model loving behaviors with your child. Talk about how real babies feel, how it is important to be careful with babies and children, and so on. Talk about how any living thing can get hurt, and how it is important to be careful of one another. This game will help you get your toddler on the right track with some very important emotional and social skills.

Naming Birds

Materials

- Spiral-bound notebook or binder with notebook paper
- Stickers
- Pencil or pen
- Encyclopedia or other research material

Spring is bird season. We see them and hear their songs. Your toddler will be excited to be introduced to the birds and learn to recognize various ones. Think about the birds in your area which are easy to identify and can be seen often enough to make playing this game possible. Some examples are . . .

Coast: sea gulls and pelicans

Midwest: robins and blue birds

Mountains: woodpeckers and eagles

Urban areas: sparrows and pigeons

Begin this educational game by designating a small, spiral notebook or binder filled with paper as your "bird book." Purchase some bird stickers or use your own drawing skills to draw small reward emblems for the book. Every time your toddler cries, "I see a birdie!" reward her with a sticker or emblem.

Naming Birds *(cont.)*

The game can be played in several other ways. For example, have a page for each bird and discover which kind of bird "wins" after a day of bird watching. Each player could also have a page; the player who spots the most birds in a day wins. If your toddler is too little to spot a specific kind of bird, simplify the game by spotting any kind of bird for a sticker.

Add to your child's knowledge base by talking about any birds you see. Make comments to your child about what the bird looks like, its special habits, and other facts you can quickly find in an encyclopedia or on the Internet. And if your toddler can tell you about a bird, give a bonus sticker.

Please and Thank You Echo Game

Materials

• None needed

Saying "please" and "thank you" is part of everyday life. It is easy to forget that manners don't come naturally to a toddler but must be reinforced again and again. Make learning to say these important words a priority with your toddler. Toddlers have a natural tendency to mimic those around them, and they also learn by repetition; both of these learning methods make this simple game a wonderful way to teach manners. It will also prevent you from later bemoaning the fact that you have a rude child on your hands.

When you go out for a walk, you might say to your toddler, "Please stay on the sidewalk. Thank you." Then have your child echo your directions, using the same polite language. Use this game to reinforce any situation where polite language is called for.

Each time you play the game and your toddler remembers to say "Please" and "Thank you," celebrate his "win" by exchanging high-fives. Say, "Great job! I love it when you use good manners. It makes me very proud of you!" It won't be long until your toddler becomes a polite child.

Water Boat Races

Materials

- Plastic boats
- Plastic wading pool, lake, or pond
- Broom, mop, or string

Collect your toddler's boats from their hiding places in toy boxes and on shelves, or buy some inexpensive plastic boats. Then take them outside and set up a boat race by filling your child's plastic wading pool with enough water to float the boats. If you are lucky enough to live by a real lake or pond, use this natural surrounding for your boat race. Remember to use safety with your toddler whenever he or she is around water—even a bucket of water can be dangerous.

One toddler can race several boats, or two or more toddlers can race one boat each. Of course, a parent can race a boat, too. There are a variety of races you can try:

- Your toddler can blow on his or her boat, or he or she can make waves in the water.

- On a windy day, see what fun the wind has in store for the little boats. Stretch a string or the pole from your mop or broom over the edge of the wading pool to form a finish line.

- Encourage your toddler to make up his or her own racing rules, and play the game again.

- If you use a wading pool, for safety's sake be sure to stay in attendance while the pool is being emptied.

Beanbag Toss

Materials

- Carton
- Waterproof paints
- Paintbrush
- Beanbags
- Scissors or craft knife

This game needs some simple preparation before it can be played. Get a large, cardboard carton from a supermarket or appliance store and cut a variety of holes in one side. Paint the box with a water-repellant paint. Paint a number next to each hole for even more fun; using numbers one, two, and three will do as your child is just beginning to have exposure to numbers.

Next, go through your toddler's toy box for bean bags. There are also a number of beanbag toys available in stores, including beanbags made in the shape of animals. You can use these toys, provided they easily fit through the holes you make in the box. If you prefer, stitch a couple of beanbags from material scraps you have around the house.

Set up the game and draw a line with chalk or tape for the player to stand behind, keeping in mind that toddlers can't throw very far. Variations of this game are numerous. You can have one or more players. You can choose one or more of the holes for a player to use. You can make a rule that before each player tosses, he or she has to say the name of the number of the hole he or she is aiming for. Or, just count the number of points accumulated by a player. This is also a game that your child can play alone; it can help to increase his or her large and small motor skills and number recognition. Remember, talking with your toddler about simple number concepts sets the stage for later learning.

Store the whole game in your garage, ready to pull out on your patio or driveway for a rousing game of beanbag toss at a moment's notice.

Guess the Shapes in Nature

Materials

- Selected items to pre-teach the shapes
- Outdoor area to explore

Take advantage of beautiful spring weather to play outdoors with your toddler by finding the shapes in nature. This game requires some pre-teaching about the basic shapes of circle, square, and triangle. Spend time with your toddler pointing out the various shapes around the house and while out on errands. Once your toddler has mastered the basics, expand his or her vocabulary by introducing other shape names such as rectangle and oval.

Then, go on a nature walk, looking for shapes in a variety of objects such as tree trunks and leaves. Here are some questions that you can ask your toddler: What do you see that is round like a circle? (a pruned shrub) What do you see is shaped like a tall triangle? (a pine tree or other evergreen) What do you see that is shaped like a rectangle? (a stone) Get your toddler to take a turn asking you questions. Also try reversing the questioning, choosing a tree or a flower and asking, "What shape is this?"

You can turn the nature walk into a more active game by having your toddler run up to the shape he sees and "tag" it with a shape name. (Be sure you play in a safe environment with no traffic around.) Not only will your toddler have fun learning the names of shapes, but he or she will get some sunshine and exercise, too.

Shell Relay Race

Materials

- Four buckets or containers
- Shells or pebbles (or leaves)
- Outdoor play area

Some May afternoon when you and your toddler could use a little fresh air, why not have a shell relay race? This is an excellent game to play at the beach or lake using shells or pebbles, but feel free to adapt this activity to use any surroundings available to you.

For this game, you will need four containers such as small sand buckets or bowls. Set up your relay race course by placing two of the containers side by side at one end, then walk the distance you wish for the course and place the other two containers in the same manner. Next, gather natural materials and place them in the containers at one end of the course; you may wish to start with only five items. Now race back and forth between the sets of containers, taking one object at a time from the container at one end and dropping it into the container at the other end. The first person to move all of her natural objects from her first bucket to her second bucket wins.

You can alter the difficulty of this game by using more objects in each bucket. You can also make the course shorter or longer depending upon the skill level of your toddler. This game is a lot of fun and it will help guarantee your toddler's nap time, too.

Rock Line Races

Materials

- Rocks
- Patio playing area or sidewalk
- Sidewalk chalk
- Box or bucket to store rocks
- Watch or kitchen timer

Children probably have been playing with rocks since the dawn of time, ever since a weary cave mother pleaded with her toddler, "Go play with your rocks!" Some things never change—children still love to play with rocks and other natural items. Provided the items are safe, let them.

Prepare for this game by gathering rocks, pebbles, or stones. You will probably find you have plenty in your garden. If you don't have a garden, search a park or lakeside area. If you live near the beach, consider playing this same game with seashells or pieces of driftwood.

After you and your toddler, or any number of rock-gatherers, have collected lots of rocks or other materials, you are ready to begin. The object of this simple game is to see who can most quickly make the longest line of rocks. Set the kitchen timer for several minutes or use your watch with a second hand to keep track of the playing time.

Another variation of this game is to use the rocks to make a shape. Draw a square on the patio or sidewalk area with sidewalk chalk and see who can fill in the square with the rocks first. You can also try outlining a shape with rocks. Use your imagination and ask your toddler to help determine the rules of the game. Another wonderful thing about games like these is that they are free and, once you gather the materials, you can play them again and again. Maybe those cave moms and dads had it pretty good, after all.

Dandelion Pick-up Game

Materials

- Lightweight bucket or other container
- Watch or kitchen timer
- Lawn full of dandelion flowers

Believe it or not, it is possible to involve your toddler in an entertaining game and get something done at the same time. The object of this game is to collect as many dandelion flowers as possible. For this game, you will need a bucket or other container for each player. Check to see that your toddler can easily lift his or her bucket or bowl before beginning.

Set the kitchen timer for five minutes and race around your lawn, collecting as many dandelions as possible before the timer goes off. While this may seem much like weeding, remember that flowers go to seed and make more dandelions. Count the dandelions after you are done; the person with the most dandelions wins. Give extra points for a dandelion flower that has gone to seed, provided the player can resist blowing the seeds all over the place!

Playing this game can give both you and your toddler the opportunity to consider other chores that can be made into games. Putting away small pieces of a building game, stashing toys in a toy basket, even tearing lettuce leaves can become a fun contest that can help you get chores done quickly.

Footprint Followers

Materials

- Sandy beach or lake area to play
- Bare feet
- Patio area and water (optional)

Toddlers love games in which they imitate their favorite people: Mommy and Daddy! Children begin mimicking their parents' behavior very early on. In fact, imitating behavior is one of the most frequent forms of early learning. This is one reason that games in which your toddler follows your examples are especially good ones.

In this game, you will lead your child on a merry chase. You will need a beach or lakeshore with moist sand in which you can create footprints. If you don't have access to a beach or lake, you can use wet feet on a patio in the summer, but you will have to work quickly so your trail doesn't disappear.

Begin by making a footprint trail. Ask your toddler to follow you. Then, make a more complex trail. Walk in small circles or form the edges of a square or other shape in the sand. Ask your toddler to follow your footsteps. If he can go from beginning to end, he wins! Then, make a footprint race course. Make two footprint paths, side-by-side. Then walk back and give the signal to "Go!" See who can make it to the end first, making sure to step in every single footstep.

Create variations of this game. Try a hopping footprint game, or use shapes in the sand as "stepping stones" to teach your toddler about simple shapes. Let your feet be your guide!

Toddler Long Jump

Materials

- Construction paper in several colors
- Tape
- Scissors
- Craft sticks
- Access to a sandy or grassy play area

Have you ever noticed that your toddler loves to run everywhere? Why does it always seem that your toddler is trying to run in the opposite direction than the one you would like? This game combines a toddler's natural ability and desire to run with jumping—an acquired skill—and adds a lot of fun to your lives. This is an especially fun game to try with a sibling who is a year or two older, but it can easily be played with just you and your toddler. Before you play, make three little flags with craft or frozen treat sticks. Cut colored paper into triangles to tape to the sticks. The stick will slide easily into the grass or sand to mark the landing spot of each jumper. Make a different color for each player and a neutral color to mark the beginning of the jumping area.

Find a grassy or a sandy area at a playground or a schoolyard that has safe, wide-open spaces away from traffic. Explain to your toddler that you are going to try a "long jump" game. Find a clear running area of 10–20 feet. Then use a flag to mark the line where you and your toddler will begin to jump. After each jump, mark the spot where the player landed. Measure the results. See who can jump the farthest and make him or her the winner. Then try the game all over again for an afternoon of easy fun.

Roly-Poly Ball

Materials

- Six tennis balls, three each of two colors
- Two different colored washable markers
- Sidewalk chalk
- Patio or other safe place to play in

This activity is something like a giant game of marbles with tennis balls standing in for the tiny round objects that pose a potential swallowing risk for your toddler.

Either purchase two cans of tennis balls or gather ones you have on hand. If possible, obtain tennis balls in two different colors to help determine whose ball is in the ring. If not, distinguish two sets of balls by using a nontoxic marker to draw colorful rings around each set of three. Let your toddler help decorate the balls, if you wish, remembering to use washable markers.

Now find a clear space on your cement patio or other area that is safe from traffic and draw a target with three rings. Label the center circle with the number three, the middle ring with a two, and the outside circle with a one.

Sit with your toddler outside the target circles and take turns rolling the tennis balls toward the center. The object, of course, is to roll a ball in the center circle as often as possible and get the most points. Play until each of you run out of tennis balls, then try again. Don't worry if your toddler doesn't understand the idea of adding points, just play the game and talk about what you are doing. This game will increase your toddler's large and small motor skills and his or her ability to follow directions and take turns.

Water Balloon Toss

Materials

- Balloons
- Plastic laundry hamper
- Water hose
- Sidewalk chalk
- Towels to dry off

Get in your bathing suits or old clothes and get ready to cool off with this exciting activity. This game will increase your toddler's coordination and large motor skills, as well provide a nice break from the afternoon heat. All you need is a package of water balloons and a water hose.

Begin this game by filling up a number of water balloons. Use a plastic laundry hamper to hold and carry the water balloons until you are ready to play (as they are slippery). Find a clear space on your backyard patio or other safe play area and use sidewalk chalk to mark 10 lines, one foot apart. You and your toddler then stand behind the first line and throw the water balloons. How far can you throw? Measure the distance with the chalk lines. The player who can throw the balloon farthest wins.

Try a variation on the game by tossing balloons back and forth to each other. In this case, the player who doesn't allow his balloon to drop wins. You will be amazed at how much fun a few water balloons can be!

Note: As with all toddler games, supervise your toddler carefully. Toddlers should never play with balloons without an adult present, and all broken balloon pieces should be disposed of immediately after the game.

Water Relay

Materials

- Bathing suit or old clothes
- Two plastic containers for each player
- Plastic cups
- Grassy area with access to water

Why do toddlers love to play in the water so much? Just like ducklings, toddlers always love to make a splash, making this water relay just the game for a warm summer day. All you need is a couple of plastic buckets, some plastic cups, and a grassy area in your yard or a park which also has access to water.

Gather two containers for each player, such as plastic sand buckets. Obtain some plastic cups; you will need to decide what size will work best for your toddler, but any plastic or paper cup that will hold water will do. Just use whatever you have around the house—no need to spend a penny.

Find a grassy area in your yard or a park in which you and your toddler can run. Then place the buckets 15–20 feet apart, farther apart for energetic toddlers, and closer for tiny tots. When you give the signal to go, you and your toddler scoop up some water from one of the buckets at one end of the course and run to the empty bucket on the other side of course, pouring water into it. The player who fills his empty bucket first wins. There are many different ways you can play this game, and the more players, the merrier, as you can have a true relay. This activity is also an excellent summer party game that is safe and inexpensive.

Bear Hospital Wagon Race

Materials

- Toy wagon
- Five to ten toy bears or dolls
- Large cardboard appliance box
- Craft knife and paints or markers (optional)

As soon as most children become old enough to know anything about medicine and healing, they begin to express an interest in doctoring their sick dollies and stuffed animals. This interest in taking care of others is a sign that a sense of empathy, or the ability to understand another's feelings, is blossoming. The appearance of empathy is a crucial emotional milestone in becoming a psychologically-healthy person. In this game your toddler will have a chance to play-act his empathy for his collection of dolls or bears.

For this game, you will need to make a pretend hospital. A pretend hospital can be as simple as a cardboard box, leaving the details up to the imagination of your child, or can be more elaborate with cutout windows and a door with a sign painted over it. You know what makes your child happy and interested—sometimes a plain old box is enough.

Bear Hospital Wagon Race *(cont.)*

Materials

- Toy wagon
- Five to ten toy bears or dolls
- Large cardboard appliance box
- Craft knife and paints or markers (optional)

Use your toddler's wagon or large truck for an ambulance. Your toddler can also pretend to be the ambulance himself and carry the dolls back and forth in his own arms. Let your toddler's imagination be your guide in creating game settings that he will enjoy.

Set up the hospital on one side of the grass and gather a few "patients" from your toddler's toy box. Now, start the game by saying, "I see some patients, ambulance driver! Can you get them to the hospital in time?" Then let your ambulance driver rescue the patients one at a time and take them to the hospital. The driver must carry the doll all the way to hospital, return and get another one, and so on, until all the dolls have been safely transported. The winner is the toddler who can achieve this task and save all his dolls or bears. Naturally, more than one player can play; players can take turns driving the ambulance or racing against each other to transporting sick dollies to the "doctor."

Slide Car Races

Materials

- Backyard or park slide
- Two or more toy cars

Zoom! In this game, toddlers will send toy cars and trucks speeding down a slide that they can imagine is a race track. This game can be played alone, with you, or with other toddlers, too.

First, select a number of cars and trucks from your toddler's toy box. For easy transport to the park, use an old duffel bag or laundry basket, although if you have a slide for your toddler in your backyard, this is ideal. Even if you don't have a slide, you can create one from a long, flat sheet of cardboard placed on an overturned box.

Begin the game by holding two cars or trucks at an appropriate distance up the slide. (Remember that you need to be just as careful with your toddler around a slide as you are with any other piece of equipment.) Give the signal to go and watch your toddler let go of the cars to see which one wins, or join your toddler and race each other's cars. You and your toddler can play this game again and again and never get tired of it.

Vary the game by trying different-sized cars and trucks. Talk about why one is faster than the other, using words such as bigger, smaller, heavier, and lighter to enhance your toddler's language skills.

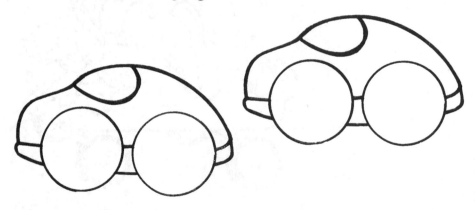

Who Is Under the Blanket?

Materials

- Grassy, shady area
- Your child's "blankie" or other blanket

This is the sort of peek-a-boo nonsense game that toddlers love to play with their parents. All you need is a blanket and your toddler to play this game. Introduce the idea of the game simply by saying, "You hide under the blanket, and I will try to guess who is there. Don't tell me it's you, but tell me just a little bit about you until I guess." Then, let your toddler give you clues about his or her identity until you guess, "It's Johnny, and here he is!" Take away the blanket and indulge in some well-deserved hugs and kisses. Your toddler will play this again and again, and so will you once you both figure out how cuddly it is!

As simple as this little game is, it will give your child the fundamental skills to play more advanced guessing games later. It will increase his verbal skills, self-confidence, and sense of autonomy as you greet him each time. You can take turns playing this game with your toddler. Try it at bedtime or in the morning, too, as a loving wake-up game.

Beanbag Balance

Materials

- Beanbag for each player
- Plastic spatula for each player (optional)
- Grassy playing area

Beanbags are an all-purpose toddler toy. This game uses beanbags to play a game that can help your toddler learn to balance her weight. If you don't have any yet, you should invest in a few as you will find you can use them again and again. Beanbags also can be made easily by cutting old material scraps into squares. Stitch two squares together, wrong sides together, leaving a small place to turn the material right-side-out. Add any type of dry beans and stitch up the hole. You may wish to double stitch homemade beanbags for extra security. (**Note:** Like all toys for toddlers, make sure beanbags are in good repair before playing since beans can be swallowed.)

Once the beanbags are ready, you can begin this balancing game in a grassy spot. Each player rests a beanbag on his or her head and tries to make it from a starting to a finish line without dropping the beanbag. Each time you do this with your toddler, her large motor skills, coordination, and balance will increase.

Try a variation of this game by adding plastic spatulas. Each player balances a beanbag on a spatula and tries to keep it there until the finish line. This is also an inexpensive and easy party game and one that your toddler can play with his or her older siblings.

Push Car Races

Materials

- Foot-powered car or tricycle
- Long ribbon or string
- Yardstick or pole
- Scarf

Do you often hear your toddler shouting, "Vroom! Vroom!" as he races around, pretending that he is a fast race car? If so, clear a space on your patio or sidewalk and get ready to race.

Begin this activity by getting out your child's foot-powered push car or tricycle. Next, tell your toddler he is going to have a car race and ask him to help you get ready. Make a starting flag by tying the edges of a scarf to a yardstick. Then use a length of leftover ribbon or piece of string to create a finish line. All you need now is a willing race car driver.

Set up the starting line and have your child get behind it on his vehicle. Give him the signal to go while you wave the flag. Let your child race to the finish line. Cheer for your child and do it again. Try a number of variations. Let your toddler's older siblings race, too, or recruit a toddler competitor and have a race for two.

Rolling Hill Races

Materials

- Comfortable, old clothes
- Low, grassy hill

Feeling agile? This game is not for the faint-of-heart or exhausted parent, but your toddler will love it. For this game, you will need to watch for grassy, low hills that will be fun to roll on at parks and other recreation areas. When you find a hill covered with soft grass and free from rocks, you will be ready to play this impromptu game. Make sure you both wear old, comfortable clothes in case of grass and mud stains.

Teach your toddler how to roll from the bottom of the slope at first. Lie down flat on your back, arms at your sides or crossed over your chest, and roll. Then hold your toddler as he practices rolling down the small slope until he feels safe and gets the hang of it. After you have both tried it a few times, try rolling by each other for a race. You will be amazed at how exhilarating this is. This game can be played anywhere you and your toddler find a safe spot. It will increase his large motor and coordination skills as well as burn off any excess energy. You will find that you are refreshed and relaxed after a little hill rolling, too. How can anyone be stressed after this kind of fun?

Sprinkler Tag

Materials

- Swimsuits
- Sunblock
- Towels
- Sprinkler
- Water hookup and hose
- Refreshing snack

Are you and your toddler stuck in a hot house—grouchy and uncomfortable? Toddlers, like most parents, become uncomfortable in the heat. This game will give you both some relief, and it doesn't cost a penny.

First, get into your swimsuits, bring out some towels, and put on sunblock. Now all you need is a sprinkler that sprays water back and forth across your yard. Set up the sprinkler so you can run back and forth while the water is moving back and forth, too.

The object of this game is to stay dry—which, of course, is impossible! Run back and forth under the spray of the sprinkler as it moves and see who can miss the water spray. You will both get wet and cool down. Soon, it won't matter who won.

After you've had enough, spread out your towel and bask in the sun for a bit, remembering to apply sun block. Take a snack out on the grass and enjoy. You and your toddler will have made a summer memory out of a hot, miserable day.

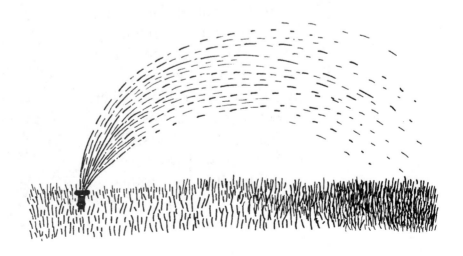

Guess the Colors

Materials

• Large box of crayons

Naming colors may be second nature to you, but this skill doesn't always come so easily to toddlers. This game will help toddlers gain familiarity with color names, but it can be adapted quickly to all levels of language development.

Start this game by using the primary colors red, blue, and yellow. For example, say, "I am looking at something red. Can you guess what it is?" Then point out what you are looking at and say to your toddler, "See the red stop sign. It's a bright red color!" Say, "I am looking at something blue, way up high! Can you guess what it is?" Then point to the sky and say, "See the blue sky? Isn't it pretty?" Use all of the primary colors first, then move on to the secondary colors of orange, purple, and green.

Once you and your toddler have perfected this game, it's time to move on to more sophisticated territory. Use "fancy" names for colors like the kind your toddler can find in her box of crayons. "Goldenrod", "magenta", and "ebony" are just a few interesting names for colors. Pick a few crayons out of your child's box each time you play to introduce the interesting color names, then look outside for items matching those colors. This color game will work well for all toddlers, no matter what their language development level.

Chalk Trail
Follow-the-Leader

Materials

- Chalk
- Playground whistle

This game will interest your toddler and be perfect for times when you have other toddlers over to play. Ideally, a parent can set up the course ahead of time, standing back later to applaud the fun while playing referee.

Draw a chalk line in, out, and around about the patio, the driveway, and the adjacent sidewalk. Be sure your playing area is free from hazards, traffic, and so on. Make the finish line somewhere with steps or a bench to sit on. Line up your toddlers, and let the leader decide on something fun to do—hop, skip, take giant steps, crawl, or some other original idea. The others follow along until you blow a playground whistle. Then the leader goes to the back of the line and the second toddler becomes the new leader. Follow up with congratulations at the end of the game. Make sure everyone gets a turn to lead.

If you are playing this game with one toddler, blow the whistle as a sign for the toddler to change actions. See how many different ones she can come up with. Give a sticker for each different action. Get ready because your toddler will probably ask to play this one again and again.

Letter Recognition Game

Materials

- Sidewalk chalk
- Candy, small prizes, and/or stickers

Give your toddler the gift of the alphabet in this easy, fun way. First, invest in a package of sidewalk chalk and put one or two pieces in your purse or pocket. Then, while you are on a walk, draw a letter on the sidewalk. If your toddler recognizes the letter, make a fuss about it. If he doesn't know its name, tell him. Say something like, "A is for apple" and repeat, drawing the letter at intervals down the sidewalk. The next time you take a walk, make a "B." Alternate the "A" and the "B" until your child can differentiate between them. Then add another letter and another on subsequent walks.

Once your toddler knows several letters, it is time to play the game. While you are taking a walk, write two or three letters with your child on the sidewalk. Say, "Which one is this?" If he can answer correctly, give him a sticker. If he doesn't pick the right one, present the letter again. Suppose you picked C-D-E the first time, and asked him to pick the "C." This time write A-B-C and ask him to pick the "C" again. In time, you will have a toddler who knows the alphabet.

Making Drippy Sand Castles

Materials

- Sand (beach or sandbox)
- Water
- Bucket

True sand castles are too hard for toddlers to build, but drippy ones are not. Drippy sand castles are simple to construct and lend themselves to competitive play between toddlers or a toddler and parent.

Drippy sand castles are made with sand and water. This is a great game for the beach, where the waves crashing against the sand makes wonderfully wet sand to use. If you can't get to the beach, you can use sand, your sand box, a bucket, and plenty of water from the hose. To make a drippy sand castle, just scoop up a wet handful of sand and let it drip between your fingers until it forms a little pile. Add to the castle by repeating the process again and again.

Start the game by having a sand castle race. Specify a time that you will both finish and admire the result. See who built a taller castle. Decide who is the winner and try it again.

Making drippy sand castles is an interesting game for toddlers and parents of all ages. You can make them as big and as fancy as you want without a lot of skill. And most toddlers are as good at this as you are!

Bubbles, Bubbles
Everywhere

Materials

- Bubble-blowing equipment
- Bubble liquid
- Play clothes

Blowing bubbles is good summertime fun for toddlers. There are all sorts of bubble-blowing equipment now on the toy market, making it easy to supply toddlers with fun things with which to blow bubbles. Here's how to make blowing bubbles into some wonderful games:

The Most Bubbles: Who can blow the most bubbles? See how high you can count. See who can count the highest, and then run around and pop them as fast as you can!

The Biggest Bubbles: Who can blow the biggest bubbles? This one takes a little more patience as you instruct your toddler on the proper way to make a big bubble. With a little practice even really young children can master this. Watch the bubbles grow bigger and bigger until . . . pop!

Chase the Bubbles: Wave a wand of bubble solution and let your child chase them around the yard. Watch as the bubbles fly off. Run after them until they disappear.

Inspect any bubble-blowing equipment you purchase before letting your child play with it. Make sure your bubble-blowing liquid is nontoxic and your toys are safe. Make sure you always cap the liquid tightly, and never suggest this game until you check your bubble liquid supply. Nothing is sadder than not having enough bubble liquid to last as long as the fun.

Ball Roll

Materials

- Balls of different sizes
- Outdoor play area with a variety of ground covers
- Net bag or beach tote

This is a game for a toddler plus mommy or daddy or for two or more toddlers with a parent referee. Each player needs a ball. Choose a small ball or a large ball— mismatched balls make the game all the more fun. You can find a variety of inexpensive balls at the grocery story and can very quickly and easily create a wonderful collection. Use a net bag or large beach tote to carry the balls in the park or other play area.

Mark a starting line and a finish line. The players roll their balls and see which one wins. Will the balls that are the same size reach the finish line together? Will a bigger ball go faster or slower than a smaller ball? Keep score, but more importantly, talk with your toddler about what is happening and why.

Carry the balls with you on a walk or in the park and use gentle slopes for your course. What happens when you roll the balls down a small slope? Try rolling the balls on the sidewalk, grass, dirt, or pavement. See what happens and share your observations with your toddler. Keep score, if your toddler wishes, and see which ball wins. Discovery is the name of this game.

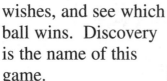

Bouncing Ball Game

Materials

- Playground ball
- Patio or other cement play area

This is the way we bounce the ball, bounce the ball, bounce the ball, so early in the morning—or the afternoon or the evening. Whenever you play this game, it will be fun for your toddler.

Get an ordinary playground ball from the supermarket or a toy store and prepare for bouncing fun. Position yourself a couple of feet away from your toddler and gently bounce the ball by throwing it down between you. When she succeeds in catching it, encourage her to bounce it to you. Gradually, increase the distance between you, and bounce the ball harder. Allow it to bounce a couple of times. Encourage your toddler to think of her own variations of the bouncing game.

This game is even more fun with two toddlers. Play "three-corner-bounce" with a parent in one corner until your toddlers get the hang of it. Then let them play the bouncing game together.

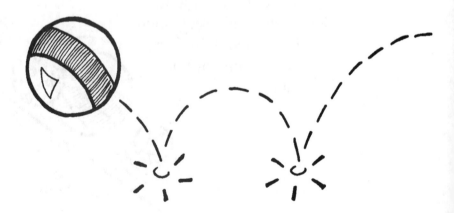

Ball in a Bucket Game

Materials

- Four plastic buckets
- Sidewalk chalk
- Four or more plastic baseballs

Put the ball in the bucket! Place it, drop it, throw it—the difficulty is up to you and your toddler. And the fun is built into the game and all its variations. Try these favorites or invent your own:

One Bucket Ball: Your toddler stands behind a line and throws the ball toward the bucket. If he makes a bucket, he gets 10 points; if he hits the bucket but the ball bounces to you, he gets five points. You can make other rules according to your toddler's skill level. Try drawing a circle around the bucket and give one point for a ball that misses the bucket, but still lands in the circle.

Four Bucket Ball: This is a great one for baseball fans and their toddlers. Place four buckets around a grassy playing area in your yard or a park to create a baseball diamond with first base, second base, third base, and home plate. Your toddler stands in the middle like a pitcher and throws to each base, trying to hit the bucket! Another variation is to run the bases and drop a ball in the bucket at each base.

Cardboard Box Basketball Game

Materials

- Two cardboard cartons
- Basketball-sized playground ball
- Patio or cement play area

Hey, basketball fans—here is a game that will give both you and your toddler a home-court advantage! Provide your toddler with two large, cardboard boxes and a basketball-size playground ball. Place the boxes at opposite ends of your patio or driveway or use a cement area in a public playground. Encourage your toddler to run up and down the court and throw the ball into the cardboard baskets.

Join your toddler on the court for a real game of one-on-one. Each of you take turns running to each cardboard box and trying to make a basket. Model the art of dribbling for your toddler and let him try it. These skills take a long time to master, but think how much fun it will be trying. Big brothers and sisters will enjoy playing, too.

Try "free throws" also. Each player stands in front of the box and shoots the ball. Do this until everyone makes a basket, then move back a step and try again. Let each player take another turn until he or she can do it. Make sure that older players play gently with your toddler and that they don't hang onto the ball. It won't be long until you have a chance to sit on the sidelines and cheer.

Do-It-Yourself Carnival Games

Materials

- Ten 2-liter, soft drink bottles
- Three beanbags for each player
- Large cardboard box

Everyone loves the kinds of games you find on a carnival midway. Here is an easy way to make your own carnival game fit for a toddler's delight. This bowling-type game recycles materials you have around the house for hours of toddler fun.

Prepare for this game by saving empty two-liter soft drink bottles, washing and drying them thoroughly. Then fill the bottles about one-third full with clean sand, beans, or anything else that will weigh the bottles enough to make them stable. After you have created 10 of these makeshift bowling pins, you will be ready to try your toddler carnival game!

Gather together the beanbags you have in the house and set up the soft drink bottles like bowling pins. You may find that you want to begin with only a few pins rather than all 10, depending on the strength of your toddler. Draw a line and let your toddler throw the beanbags at the bottles until he knocks them down.

You can make the game more challenging, and introduce number concepts, by printing a number on each bottle with a thick marking pen. Count the points and add up the score. When you are through with this game, pile the pins in a cardboard box and store them in your garage until your toddler wants to play again.

Clothing Relay

Materials

- Grassy playing area
- Old clothes
- Socks
- Hats

This game is fun for one or more toddlers. Toddlers begin by selecting a piece of clothing at the starting line, putting it on, then racing to the finish line. Design the game to "suit" your toddler. Look at these examples and choose your favorite, or try them all.

Hat Relay: Have a selection of hats ready for your toddler (or toddlers) to try on. Place the pile of hats across the yard. Then have each toddler run to the pile, select a hat, put it on, and run back. The toddler who makes it back to the starting line with a hat on his or her head wins!

Sock Relay: Try this fun relay to help toddlers practice putting on their socks. Have a pile of socks waiting for your toddler (or toddlers) to put on. Players run to the pile, sit down, pull on the socks, and then run back. Make it more complicated by insisting players have matching socks!

Get Dressed Relay: This is the ultimate clothing relay race. Have your toddler (or toddlers) dressed in a swimsuit. Each player runs to the selection of clothes and "gets dressed." The first player dressed wins! This relay will help children learn to put on their clothes by making the process fun.

Which Is Heavier?

Materials

- Sets of things to compare
- Outdoor area to explore
- Hose or drinking fountain
- Plastic, soft drink bottle

Which is heavier, a sock or a leaf? an orange or a flower? Let your toddler experiment in this simple game to find out which object is heavier. Soon, she will be learning logic and some of the basic skills she will later use in school when studying science.

Start by talking with your toddler about whatever you happen to see in your backyard or park. Pick up a flower and a rock and ask her which is heavier. Let her hold each item and try to figure it out. If your toddler is right a certain number of times, give her a small prize.

Repeat the activity using a plastic, soft drink bottle and water from a hose or drinking fountain. Ask your toddler which one is heavier—a bottle filled with water or one that is empty? Let your toddler have hands-on experience with this after she has made her initial guess, or hypothesis. Who knows? You may find you have a junior scientist on your hands. Try this again with several children; the child who guesses correctly is the winner.

Bigger or Smaller Than Me

Materials

• An outdoor area to explore

When you're out on your next walk with your toddler, get him to pick out things that are bigger or smaller than he is. Let him do this five times to win a prize. Get another toddler or an older sibling to try it, too, to make this activity even more fun.

Some "bigger than me" ideas could include . . .

• stop sign
• police officer or fire fighter
• building
• car
• truck
• big kids on bikes

Some "smaller than me" ideas could include . . .

• bugs
• butterflies
• leaf
• rock
• kitten, puppy, or other small animal
• flowers
• newspaper

When your toddler can tell you five things that are bigger or smaller than he is, praise him and try it again. This is also a good game for long road trips or while waiting in line.

Leaf Collecting and Sorting Game

Materials

- Leafy area to explore
- Plastic bucket

It's October and the leaves in most places are changing colors. Gather some leaves and let your toddler turn them into a leaf-sorting game. Try this game several different ways to see which one your toddler likes the best.

Sorting by Color: Your toddler can sort any collection of fall leaves by color. In your yard or a park with lots of fallen leaves, have your toddler make piles of different colors. Start out by finding only red leaves, then yellow, green, and brown. Make up different rules as you go along. Maybe the first player who finds a handful of red leaves wins, or maybe it will be the first player to find an orange one.

Sorting by Shape: The same leaves that you and your toddler sorted by color can be used again to sort by shape. Look for oval, pointed, and serrated shapes. See if your toddler can find broken leaves that look like other shapes, like squares, triangles and more. See who can find the first pointed leaf or the first leaf with more than one point. Make up rules for this game based on the differences you see in the leaves around you.

Bring a plastic bucket and carry some leaves home to press. Make a leaf collection, or sort them again. Put leaves of many colors in a bucket, pour them out, and sort as fast as you can.

Note: Be careful to supervise the kinds of leaves your toddler plays with. Be aware of poisonous varieties that grow around your area, and make sure everyone washes his or her hands after the game.

Animal Sounds

Materials

• None needed

Are you in the car with an energetic toddler? Or are you waiting somewhere with no end in sight? Now is a perfect time for the Animal Sounds Game. In this game you will get a chance to see if your toddler can recognize the basic animal sounds. If she can't, this is a great way to teach her.

Begin this game by seeing which sounds your toddler knows. Say, "What animal says 'moo'?" When your toddler answers, "Cow!", go on to another sound. Make sure she has a repertoire of sounds before proceeding to the next Animal Sounds Game.

In a variation of this game, your toddler says, "What goes 'moo'?" and you or another toddler answers. Give points, stickers, or applause for a job well done. Here is a list of some common animal sounds to get you started:

"*Meow,*" goes the cat.

"*Roar,*" goes the lion.

"*Quack,*" goes the duck.

"*Bark,*" goes the dog.

"*Cluck,*" goes the hen.

"*Honk,*" goes the goose.

"*Baa,*" goes the sheep.

"*Cock-a-doodle-doo,*" goes the rooster.

If you happen to spot any of these animals on a car trip, that is a perfect opportunity to give this game a try.

We Are Thankful for Many Things

Materials

• None needed

In November we become more aware of the many things for which we are thankful. Use the holiday mood to inspire a little thankfulness in your toddler. This game is a wonderful one, and it will make you count your blessings, too.

Begin by talking about being grateful. Tell your toddler the things for which you are grateful, such as your home, your family, a special talent, or a beautiful sunset. Encourage your toddler to think about the things for which he or she is grateful. You may have to try this often for your toddler to get the hang of it. Take turns with your toddler naming things or people you are grateful for. Keep going until one person can't think of anything else.

Try organizing the things for which you are grateful around a central topic, such as things in nature or even household items. This game will encourage you to talk with your toddler and listen to what he or she thinks. This is an excellent game to play while in the car or waiting somewhere which can get tedious for both you and your toddler.

Shopping List Game

Materials

- Access to a grocery store
- Paper
- Pencil or pen
- Shopping circular (optional)

Have you ever wanted an assistant to help you with the tedious and exhausting chores you do everyday? Well, you do have one, and guess who it is? That's right, it's your toddler! In this game your child is asked to identify and find an object in the grocery store. This game will help your toddler identify objects, expand his vocabulary, and learn to follow simple directions.

Begin by asking your child to help you shop. If you wish, you can look through the grocery section of your newspaper or other weekly store circular delivered in the mail. This way you can explain to your child what you want to buy, as well as show him a picture of the item. Then make two lists—a regular shopping list for you and a separate list for your toddler containing three items written in large letters. The object of the game is for your child to find all of the things on his list. Decide ahead of time what his prize for helping will be; some grocery stores give children a free balloon or cookie, and this can be an economical prize.

Once in the store, help your child look for his items. As he finds each one, add it to the basket. Talk with your child about the items you see and help your child cross off the found items on his list with a pencil. Remember, toddler games should be easy to win. If you play this one often enough, eventually you will have a talented assistant.

Nature Alphabet Hunt

Materials

- Access to a library
- Library card
- ABC books

Letter recognition is a skill you can begin to teach your toddler very early on. Later, when your toddler is old enough for school, you will be glad you did. Begin by talking about the alphabet with your toddler. Use any of the colorful ABC books published to familiarize your child with the letters.

Begin this game by taking a trip to the library with your child. Pick out an ABC book to read at the library, possibly checking it out to take home. After you have read the book, pick a letter and begin letter recognition. At the start of this activity, don't expect your toddler to be able to name anything that begins with the letters. At this point, you are only interested in introducing a letter.

As you leave the library, decide to look for any letter at all. Ask your child to point out any letter he or she recognizes, responding with praise for correct answers and gently correcting wrong guesses. Make the game more interesting by asking your child to find three letters all at once. After completing this task, use a small reward to celebrate the excitement of learning to identify letters.

The City Guessing Game

Materials

• Access to a city location

Not all outdoor games involve nature. Some of the most interesting things a toddler can see outdoors are part of urban surroundings. Toddlers love the noise, movement, color, and smells of big machines. This game takes you into your city with your toddler. It can be played again and again, using different city surroundings.

First, decide where you are going to go. The only criteria is that the urban surrounding you pick must have lots of fascinating things to see. If your child already has a special attraction to something, like trucks or skyscrapers, use this as your guide. Otherwise, use the ideas below as suggestions:

- police station
- construction site
- downtown areas with skyscrapers
- factory sites
- train or bus station
- airport

Go to the selected location with your toddler and talk about what you see. For example, if you go to a train station, look at the trains and talk about them. Try to observe (or even meet) some train personnel. Notice as much as you can and then play the guessing game. Say, "I am thinking of something that goes 'choo-choo'! Can you guess what it is?" Complete this game many times with many different objects in each situation. Remember to praise your child for correct answers. You will be amazed at how this simple game will act as a learning tool for your toddler and provide a lot of entertainment, too.

Holiday Shopping Hunt

Materials

- List of people for whom to buy gifts
- Dollar for each person on the list
- Local dollar-discount store

It's almost holiday time, and that means time to start your toddler thinking about giving as well as receiving. Talk with your toddler about buying Christmas, Hanukkah, or Kwanza presents. Then tell her you are going to take her to a store where she can pick out something for everyone on her list.

There are many dollar-discount stores that can be an excellent place to give your child a chance to do her own shopping. If you don't have a dollar-discount store near you, try a garage sale or a sidewalk sale. Let your toddler pick out one present for each person on the list. She can get a lovely vase for grandma, cookies for her brothers, and costume jewelry for sisters. Reward her with praise for making good decisions; she wins the game by finding something for everyone in her family.

As you play games such as this one with your toddler, you will begin to notice that your child thinks about what she can give as well as what she will receive—and isn't that a lovely thought for any holiday?

Cookies and Candies Outdoor Race

Materials

- Cookies, already frosted
- Candies
- Plastic bowls
- Outdoor picnic or card table
- Paper plates

Nothing gets messier than kids decorating cookies, which is why this game is played outdoors. This game works well when you have more than one toddler playing or a toddler with an older sibling.

Begin by buying or baking some plain cookies. Frost the cookies with white frosting and set aside. Set up a card or picnic table outside. Use paper plates to hold cookies for each player. Then give each toddler playing an ice tray, muffin tin, or small bowl filled with a variety of candy pieces.

When you give the signal to go, the toddlers are to fill up their cookies with the candies. Have "winners" eat their prize, or do this a number of times to make cookies for Santa or for a holiday dessert.

Be sure to use soft candies that are easy to chew. Make sure that you supervise this and any other game in which a child is using small objects.

Some easy-to-eat candies and treats include . . .

- sprinkles
- alphabet cereal
- round oat cereal
- chocolate chips
- candy coated chocolate pieces
- gummy critters
- gum drops

Outdoor Tree Trimming Race

Materials

- Small tree or branch
- Plastic, wooden or papier mâché ornaments
- bread-dough ornaments
- ribbons and bows
- candy canes
- two or three small boxes to cover decorations

Show your toddler the collection of ornaments and explain that you are going to play "hide and seek" with him or her to decorate the small tree or branch.

Hide the first ornament under one of the boxes and ask him or her to find it.

Everytime he or she finds an ornament, he or she can put it on the tree.

An ornament can be put under one box or both, depending on the age and frustration level of the child. Celebrate with cookies and juice as you view the wonderful new addition to the holiday decor.

Dreidel Pro Game

Materials

- Dreidel
- Candies
- Stickers

Toddlers with older siblings have the constant dilemma of trying to keep up, which can be upsetting. This game allows you to give your toddler a head start so that when he plays with older children he already will have somewhat perfected his skill.

Show your toddler how to use a dreidel, or small spinning top. Give him a sticker every time he can actually make the dreidel spin. Have lots of small candy prizes of stickers on hand to make the game fun. You can do this game any time of year to ensure that by Hanukkah he is a pro at spinning the dreidel.

You can discuss with your toddler the position in which the dreidel lands and explain the symbols if he is interested. You will know when he is ready to learn the real game and challenge the older children in your house.

What's in the Shopping Bag?

Materials

• None needed

The holidays make a wonderful setting for outdoor games you can play with your toddler. There is so much to see as you drive or walk around town—colors, lights, and cheery decorations. Why not use these for a wonderful memory game that will help you and your toddler get in the spirit of Christmas or Hanukkah quickly? (If it is appropriate for your family's beliefs, you can play this game as "What's in Santa's Sack?")

"What's in the Shopping Bag?" is a game you can play with any toddler who is beginning to understand the concept of holiday shopping and giving. While the game is meant to be entertaining, it also increases memory and language skills—both important skills that will be helpful later in school.

Begin this game by modeling it. Say, "Let's play a fun game. When I see something while we are shopping that I think would be a lovely gift, I put it in a pretend shopping bag in my imagination. Like this: I see a beautiful dolly. I'll put the dolly with the blonde hair in the shopping bag. When I see something else I like, I'll remember what I put in first and then put in the next thing. I'll say, 'I'll put the blonde dolly and the red truck in the shopping bag. I can keep doing this as long as I see things I want, and the fun part is trying to remember everything I said I wanted to put in the shopping bag. Let's try it together, and then we can remind each other about the things that we pretend to put into the shopping bag."

Indoor Games

Bedroom Games

Anywhere Games

Guess Which Room
I Am In

Materials

• Your kitchen and its contents

Acquaint your toddler with the kitchen by using a simple guessing game. Toddlers love such games, and just by participating they seem to increase their language skills by the minute.

Begin by taking a look at your own kitchen. Kitchens are amazing places for toddlers. There are so many interesting tools and machines that move and make noises—as well as things that must not be touched. To make your kitchen as safe a place to explore as possible, make sure that knives and other dangerous objects are out of the way. Check underneath your cabinets to make sure no poisonous cleaning supplies can be reached either. Finally, check outlets and make sure they are covered with child-safe plug covers.

Now make note of the kinds of things you have that are commonly found in kitchens, such as the following:

• pots
• pans
• large serving spoons
• plastic containers of all sizes
• sink

• dish towels
• paper towels
• gadgets
• measuring tools
• plastic cups

Tell your toddler that you are going to say some clues about a special room in your house to see if he can guess what room it is. Go through the process of giving clues until your child correctly guesses the room. Follow up the guessing game by looking in the kitchen together and discussing all of the things you gave as clues. Then play the rest of the games in this section.

Measuring Game

Materials

- Collection of miscellaneous measuring tools
- Water or a supply of rice
- Blanket or sheet

On a day when you are cleaning your kitchen cupboards and drawers, get out all of your metal and plastic measuring tools for your toddler to play with. With a little help from you, these tools can turn into a great game.

Before playing, decide if your toddler will be measuring water or a dry substance. If the weather is hot and the floor can use washing, put your toddler on a chair at the kitchen sink to measure with water. If not, spread a blanket or sheet on the floor and let your toddler measure with grains of rice.

The easiest measuring game is to ask your toddler to find out how many measures a large container will hold. Give your toddler both a large and small empty container. Encourage your toddler to guess how many times he can measure and pour water or rice from the small container into the large container, then let him experiment. If your toddler is right, give him a hug and a large amount of praise. If your toddler misses, it's time to try again. There are endless variations of this game—let your collection of containers be your guide.

Shopkeeper Game

Materials

- Unbreakable and unopened food items
- Toy shopping cart
- Toy cash register
- Collection of money, play or real

What is more fun than setting up a grocery store? And what better place to stock your toddler's pretend store than in your kitchen?

Your toddler can find all of his favorite foods right in your cupboards, or you might want to set aside one shelf in your cupboard and allow your miniature storekeeper to choose from items you keep there. You can stock this with unbreakable food items such as boxes of gelatin and instant puddings, unopened packages of cereal, small cans of fruits and vegetables, and cake and frosting mixes.

You can collect all kinds of props for this game, such as a toy shopping cart and cash register. You can also provide play money or real coins for the shoppers to use. Once you are set up, let your toddler select items for the store. If you have two toddlers playing this game, you might want to let them take turns shopping and selling, or you can be the shopper.

Shopkeeper Game *(cont.)*

Materials

- Unbreakable and unopened food items
- Toy shopping cart
- Toy cash register
- Collection of money, play or real

Additional game ideas:

- Provide a grocery bag. Have your toddler race against the clock to fill it up.

- Have your toddler sort the foods into items for breakfast, lunch, and dinner.

- Have one or two toddlers group the foods back on the pantry shelf.

- You can also pretend to be the shopkeeper and let your toddler choose and pay for items to the best of her abilities. Toddlers who have a habit of rejecting your dinner choices might be more agreeable to tasting foods they have shopped for themselves.

Alphabet Game

Materials

- Cardboard
- Marking pens
- Supplies of food representing letters of the alphabet

The kitchen is a good place to introduce the alphabet. With a little effort, you can turn the whole alphabet into play while you go about your daily tasks.

To start, make large alphabet cards for your toddler using block letters, beginning with Aa and ending with Zz. Start by showing your toddler the Aa card, then have her find a food that begins with that letter in your kitchen. Canned or packaged foods will be easiest since they have the letters right on them. (You may wish to purchase some foods in order to cover all the letters. A can of kumquats will take care of Kk, and a jar of quince jelly will take care of Qq. You're on your own for Xx, however.) Use stickers as rewards; educational supply stores may even have stickers with fruits and vegetables or other foods on them.

Alphabet Game *(cont.)*

Materials

- Cardboard
- Marking pens
- Supplies of food representing letters of the alphabet

Here is a list of some possible alphabet-friendly foods so that you can give your toddler some clues to finding correct matches:

applesauce	oatmeal
beans	peanut butter
coffee	quince jelly
dates	rice
eggs	sugar
flour	tea
grapefruit juice	upside-down cake
honey	vanilla extract, vanilla pudding
ice cream	water
jam, jelly	x_____?
kumquats	yeast
lemonade mix	zucchini
marmalade	
nuts	

Plastic Container Toss

Materials

- Plastic containers of various sizes
- Beanbag toys
- Masking tape
- Pen
- Stickers or small prizes

Rainy, indoor days are perfect for a game of plastic container toss. Gather your plastic storage containers and beanbag toys from your toddler's toy box, or make a set of beanbags (See page 50.). Using masking tape and a marker, label your collection of containers with a target score: five points for wide containers, 10 for medium containers, and 20 for narrow containers. Set the containers in a line, then use masking tape to mark a throw line on the floor. Each player should toss all of the beanbag toys, adding up the score with an adult's help. Give all the players a small prize or sticker for effort.

There is a variation of this game for the littlest toddler: just choose one plastic tub—a large one—and have your toddler toss in beanbags. For every toy she gets in, she gets a point. Five successful throws can earn the child a small prize or sticker.

Choo-Choo Train Game

Materials

- Cans and boxes from your cupboards

Who can make the longest train out of cans and packaged foods? This is a great game for your toddler to play while you clean out your cupboards and rearrange your supplies. If you have two toddlers who can play together, they can compete. If you have only one toddler playing, he or she can make one train of cans and one train of boxes to see which is the longest.

Try changing the words and fitting your child's name into the song "Little Red Caboose" for example:

> *Little Danny's choo-choo!*
> *Little Danny's choo-choo!*
> *Little Danny's choo-choo goes 'round the room, room, room, room.*
> *Boxes for its stack, stack, stack, stack,*
> *Coming 'round the track, track, track, track,*
> *Little Danny's choo-choo goes 'round the room—toot, toot!*

When you are through wiping down the cupboards, ask the "engineer" to drive the train and put everything back where it belongs.

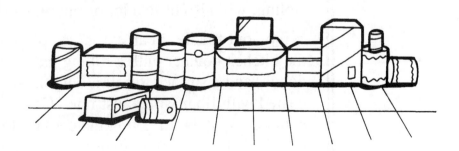

Cookie Dough and Rolling Pin Game

Materials

- Prepared cookie dough
- Rolling pin
- Cookie cutters in various shapes
- Floured surface, such as a bread board
- Spatula
- Apron

What toddler doesn't like to squish and scrunch something with a rolling pin? If that something should be cookie dough, it's more fun than ever. In this game you teach your toddler to identify and make basic shapes and then eat the results.

Begin by looking over your cookie cutters. You will need a round one, a square one, and a triangular one. Finding a round cookie cutter is fairly easy, but don't worry if you can't find the other shapes; you can easily cut squares and triangles, using a dull plastic or butter knife.

Begin by showing your child circle, square, and triangle shapes. Then ask him to help you make some shape cookies. Start by making the shapes for your toddler and seeing if he can name them. Then, ask him to try to make the shapes himself. This will probably take some time because toddlers are just beginning the process of mastering the eye-hand coordination required to do this task.

Vary the game by using other shapes you have and playing "guess the shape." You might have seasonal or character cookie cutters which will all work as nice game variations. Two toddlers, or a toddler and an older sibling, will also have a lot of fun playing this game.

Wrap your toddler in an apron and place him on a chair at the kitchen counter with a rolling pin, a supply of cookie dough, and a surface to roll it out on. A breadboard coated with flour works just fine. Give him cookie cutters, a spatula for lifting the cookies to the baking pan, and the help in learning to use these items. After you are all done, make sure to enjoy the results.

Salt and Flour Dough Games

Materials

- Salt and flour dough
- Rolling pin
- Work area
- Plate for finished products
- Cookie cutters (optional)

What if you love your toddler but just don't want the mess of baking cookies? Move your toddler to a corner of the kitchen, break open your supply of play dough, and let him create a plate of mouth-watering faux cookies for your dinner dessert.

Set up the rules for this game ahead of time: The cookies may or may not look like real cookies. They should, however, look good enough to eat. When they are finished, they should be set attractively on a plate. If anyone in the house reaches for one, the toddler earns a point. If anyone gets the cookies halfway to his or her mouth, the toddler earns five points. Anyone who actually starts to bite into one earns the toddler 10 big points. Another variation of this game will give you the time you need to cook dinner and keep an eye on your toddler. Give your toddler three to five cookie cutters. Explain that the challenge is to roll out the dough and make a cookie using each cookie cutter. This should keep your toddler busy to give you enough time to start dinner.

Salt and Flour Dough Recipe

Mix equal parts of flour and salt thoroughly. Add water, a little bit at a time, until the dough is of the right consistency, like cookie dough. Color dough with different colors of food coloring. Store any leftovers in airtight plastic containers.

Weighing Things

Which is heavier, a 1-lb. can of shortening or a 1-lb. package of butter or margarine? A 2-lb. bag of pasta or a 2-lb. can of coffee? Let your toddler find out by weighing familiar things in your kitchen.

For this game, set up a panel of items to test, for instance, a 1-lb. can of shortening; a 2-lb. bag of pasta; a candy bar; and an unbreakable bottle of pancake syrup. Then allow your toddler to choose things from your cupboard and refrigerator that might weigh the same as the items you selected. You need only a bathroom scale to weigh things, although you may wish to use a balance scale if you have one.

Your toddler can start by weighing the shortening. You can gently guide him to weigh the butter next so he will succeed at the outset. Let him go through your cupboards, or suggest possibilities you want him to consider. For every correct match, celebrate with a hug and praise.

This game will provide for some interesting exchanges between you and your toddler. The fact that shape has no influence upon weight (shortening and butter) and size has no influence upon weight (pasta and coffee) can result in some meaningful and interesting conversations.

Following Directions

Materials

- 1 package instant pudding mix
- 2 cups milk
- Wire whisk
- Dessert dishes

How can you create a game for following directions? By using ready-to-mix instant pudding, that's how! It's safe, it's cool, and it's yummy.

Set your toddler up with ingredients, implements, and directions. Each correctly-followed direction earns praise for your toddler. You can give a sticker for a job well done or simply a pat on the back.

Vary the game by having a competition for cleanup, too. Give your toddler a sponge and a section of kitchen counter space to wipe off. Now you or a sibling can take another section of counter space. The winner is the person who gets his or her own counter area the cleanest.

Directions:

1. Pour two cups (480 mL) of milk into medium bowl.

2. Add pudding mix.

3. Beat with wire whisk for two minutes.

4. Pour at once into dessert dishes.

5. Serve any time after five minutes.

Make-a-Face Rice Cake Snack

Materials

- Cream cheese or peanut butter
- Assorted fruits or vegetables
- Rice cakes

Toddlers love to handle food. This easy activity gives them a chance to do just that, while they create a work of art that can be eaten.

Spread a rice cake with cream cheese or peanut butter. For a sweet face snack, cut up fruits to use as facial features. Cherry halves, blueberries, raisins, and so forth can be used as eyes. Bits of strawberry or pieces of red fruit roll-up can be used for the mouth. A bit of banana or apple can become a nose. Dried apricots or pears can be affixed to the side for ears.

For a savory snack, use tomatoes, cucumber slices, shredded carrot, celery pieces, and so forth to make facial features. Use mushroom slices for ears and bits of red pepper for a mouth.

When you are finished, take photographs of the results before you eat them.

Make-a-Face Rice Cake Snack *(cont.)*

Toddler Taste Test

Materials

- Blindfold
- Assorted common foods
- A tray

Set up a toddler version of a blindfold taste test to educate your toddler's taste buds. Give her tiny tastes of common foods to sharpen her perceptions. Reward correct answers with cheers.

What shall you give your blindfolded toddler? Some good choices are milk, sugar, salt, orange juice, apple juice, soda crackers, graham crackers, chocolate pudding, ice cream, carrots, toast, or anything you are going to have for lunch. Who knows? She may discover she likes some foods she once rejected.

Begin the game by explaining to your toddler that you are both going to play a food guessing game. Have a tray prepared with at least four, possibly six foods on it. One player picks a food and gives it to the other player, who is blindfolded, and sees if she can guess the food. The player who guesses correctly the most number of times wins.

You can set up this game in two ways: Let your toddler see everything from which you will select or hide everything from her. It's fun either way.

Guess Which Room
I Am In

Materials

- Your bathroom and everything in it

Acquaint your toddler with the bathroom by using a simple guessing game. Toddlers love such games, and just by participating, they seem to increase their language skills by the minute.

Begin by thinking about the kinds of things you would find in any bathroom. There is a bathtub or a shower, a toilet (or a potty), a sink, towels and a waste paper basket. Think of other things you might find: soap, bubble bath, make-up, combs, and brushes. Try checking your own bathroom for unique items before beginning this guessing game.

Tell your toddler that you are going to say some clues about a special room in your house to see if he can guess what room it is. Go through the process of giving clues until your child correctly guesses the room. Then suggest a quick trip to the bathroom to see and discuss all of the things that you gave as clues. This will help your toddler name objects for which he is still uncertain. Then play the rest of the games in this section.

Buckets of Fish

Materials

- Plastic fish
- Two toy buckets or plastic bowls
- Bathtub full of water
- Bubble bath (optional)
- Constant supervision!

Feel like fishing in your bathtub? Sounds like a terrible clean-up job! But not if you use plastic or rubber fish. You can find plastic fish in most toy departments of almost any kind of store. However, if you have trouble, a toy store that specializes in educational toys will probably have what you want.

For this game, you will need a bathtub full of water. Your toddler can be either in the tub taking a bath or outside the tub.

Note: Always watch your toddler around water in a bathtub, toilet, or sink. Toddlers can quickly drown by falling head-first into even a small amount of water.

Next, you will need two plastic buckets. The kind you find in toy stores will work fine. If you don't have buckets on hand, you can always use two plastic bowls from your kitchen. Just make sure anything you handle in the bathroom is plastic and can't break.

Now, you and your toddler can pour the fish into the water. Each of you gets to catch the plastic fish by reaching into the water, grabbing the fish with your hands and putting them in your own bucket. The person who catches the most fish wins.

You can make this especially interesting and exciting by adding bubble bath to the water—pretend you are in Alaska ice fishing!

Soap Paint Fun

Materials

- Nontoxic soap paint
- Your bathtub full of water and your toddler
- Constant supervision!

For some unfortunate reason, toddlers love to write on walls. Here is a game to give your artist an outlet for his creativity and save your walls, too.

There are a variety of nontoxic bathroom soap paints that you can purchase at the toy store. You can also sometimes find these soap paints with bath products in a drug store. Soap paints can be used to write on the walls of your bathroom and can then be washed off. They are perfect for practicing letters of the alphabet in this guessing game.

After introducing your toddler to the alphabet, write a soap letter on the wall and ask him to tell you its name. Repeat this exercise with another letter. Each time your child guesses a letter, he wins a point. As he gets a bit older, he will be able to write the letters himself. If he can copy a soap letter you write, he wins again.

Finally, teach him to read his name and your name, and then the names of other family members. Every time he can read a name, he wins. You can think up many ways to play with soap paint using your imagination. Each time you play, your child learns the reading readiness skills he will need for preschool and kindergarten.

Make the Best Hairdo

Materials

- Gentle, tear-free shampoo
- Your bathtub full of water and your toddler
- Constant supervision!

You look mah-vah-lous, darling! Your toddler and his or her dollies will be able to say the same after playing this fun, shampoo hairdo game. The game is sure to be hands-on, soapy fun for both of you. All you need are several of your toddler's dolls with long hair. Be sure to pick older dollies that you won't mind having look a little untidy once this activity is over.

Using your child's tear-free shampoo, help your toddler give his or her dolly a great head of lather. You can wash another doll's hair at the same time. Use the soapy shampoo mixture to shape the doll's hair into different, interesting styles. You can also do this with your toddler's hair and shampoo his or her hair at the same time. (Take a few camera shots to keep some fun memories.)

After you and your toddler have each created hairstyles for the dolls, decide which is the most beautiful, the funniest, the most unusual, etc. Decide upon categories to judge the dollies' hairstyles and try it again. Everyone wins in this game because your toddler ends up being happy and clean and actually enjoys getting his or her hair shampooed.

Sink or Float Soap Game

Materials

- Several bars of soap
- One bar of original Ivory® soap
- One bathtub full of water and your toddler
- Plastic or other safe container
- Constant supervision!

This game makes your toddler's bath time a science lesson. All you need is one toddler and several bars of soap.

Before your toddler has begun to bathe, show him the different soaps you have either purchased at the store or collected on vacation. You might even involve your toddler in a shopping trip to the supermarket to select several bars of soap. However you acquire your soaps, be sure to include a bar of original Ivory® soap because it is the one soap that is certain to float.

Let your child help you unwrap bars of soap and place them all in a safe container in easy reach before you and your toddler begin her bath. Each of you selects a bar of soap and drops it in the water. The person whose soap floats, wins. You can also play that the person whose soap sinks, wins; the rule is up to you. Make it more of an experiment and discuss which soap might float and why before you drop it in the water. Your toddler will have an interesting time and can't help but get clean.

Soap Boat Race

Materials

- Two new bars of original Ivory® soap
- Two plastic forks
- Two pieces of paper
- Tape
- Scissors
- Crayons

While you are out buying soap for the previous game, you might as well get another couple of bars. This time around, you and your toddler will make and race your very own soap boats. This activity is easy to do and requires minimal preparation.

You will need two new bars of original Ivory® soap. Get out your art supplies and make two paper sails from any type of paper. Decorate the sails with crayons if you like. Make the mast from a plastic, disposable fork. Tape the sail to the fork, then stick the fork tines into the soap. You are ready to race.

Fill the bathtub and have each player place her boat at one end of the tub to begin. See what happens. Decide upon a finish line and declare a winner. You may have to experiment by fanning your boats along or perhaps waving your hands gently in the water behind the boats to make them go. Another way to create a current is to run the water gently and have the area under the faucet be the takeoff point for the race. You and your toddler can try this again any day you wish. Just save your plastic forks and make new sails.

How Many?

Materials

- Plastic bowls, cups, and measuring equipment
- Your bathtub full of water and your toddler
- Constant supervision!

You probably never thought of combining a bathtub with early math and science learning, but you can. This game gives you an opportunity to introduce your toddler to measurement, estimation, and counting—all important math and science skills.

Begin by gathering the materials you will need and placing these in reach of the bathtub before you run the water. Your toddler can help with this preparation. Get a plastic bowl, measuring cups, and spoons from the kitchen or you can use any empty, plastic container from your bathroom to experiment as well.

Once your child is in the tub, give her the plastic bowl and ask her to guess how many cups of water it will it take to fill up the bowl. Then let her fill the bowl, counting cups as she does. A correct guess wins. Take turns guessing and filling. Try filling different size containers with different size cups. There are many variations to this game.

Enhance the learning experience by using words that will acquaint your toddler with the world of science and math. Some words to use might include the following:

- more
- full
- guess
- right
- how many
- less
- empty
- estimate
- correct

Learning to Blow Bubbles Game

Materials

- Your bathtub full of water
- A towel for each player
- Constant supervision!

Water safety can and should begin in the bathtub. In this game you can teach your toddler to put her face in the water and safely blow bubbles. It's important for your child to approach water with the proper attitude, that is, enjoying it but also respecting it. Using this approach, you can set the stage for a whole lifetime of good water experiences.

For this game, all you will need is a bathtub full of water and a couple of towels. (Since you will be putting your face in the water while you are dressed, you might want to wear old, comfy clothes.) You and your toddler kneel at the side of your bathtub. Ask your toddler if he can blow out air, and demonstrate what you mean before putting your faces in the water. Get your toddler to demonstrate blowing air to the count of three.

When your child is comfortable, ask her to play the "blowing bubbles game" with your face in the water. See who can blow the most bubbles. See who can blow bubbles to a count of three. You and your toddler will be able to make up variations to this game as you go along.

Be sure to talk about water safety with your child. Let her know she should never turn on the bathtub water or get in the bathtub unless an adult is in the bathroom, too. As always, remember water safety begins with the attitude you model.

Which Part Am I Scrubbing?

Materials

- Your bathtub full of water and your toddler
- Constant supervision!

In this game, you teach your toddler to recognize the words for the parts of his body. Learning the word names for objects is an early and crucial part of language development. In this game all you need is your toddler in his bath.

Begin by learning this simple song, sung to the tune of "Row, Row, Row Your Boat," substituting your child's name:

> *Scrub, scrub, scrub-a-dub,*
> *Scrubbing in the tub.*
> *Can you tell me what's being scrubbed,*
> *And help me sing along?*
> *Scrub, scrub, scrub-a-dub,*
> *Scrubbing in the tub*
> *Mommy's scrubbing Timmy's* _____,
>   *(name of body part)*
> *Scrubbing in the tub.*

Ask your child to guess the name of the part of his or her body being scrubbed to win. When your child doesn't know a word, supply it and try the game again. Then, vary the game by having your child try it with his eyes closed. Soon bath time will be over and your child will have increased his vocabulary, too.

Who's in There?

Materials

- Your bathtub full of water and your toddler
- Towels
- Baby powder
- Constant supervision!

Sooner or later, you have got to get your toddler out of the bathtub no matter how much he loves to splash in the water. When you do finally convince him to get out, why not play this cuddly drying game? Have dry towels and powder right by the bathtub before you begin.

Begin by giving your toddler a long, enjoyable bath. Afterwards, while you are drying your toddler, place the towel gently over his head and play this simple guessing game as you gently rub your toddler's hair, saying:

Who's in there?
Baby Bear!

This may sound extremely simple, but sometimes the best games are, especially with a very young toddler just learning to talk. You can personalize and insert your toddler's name in front of the word "bear." Your toddler wins this one by being able to reply to your question with the phrase that you teach him. This simple game can be played different ways according to your child's imagination (and yours).

This game will help your child understand that he is a separate individual. It is also a sure way to get a few hugs—perhaps the healthiest reason of all to play this game.

Pick-up Pals

Materials

- Bath toys
- Two plastic buckets with handles
- A child-safe toy storage space
- Constant supervision!

Tired parents agree that it is never too early to begin teaching a child to clean up after herself. While a toddler cannot be expected to master this skill, she can be introduced to it at an early age.

For this game, you will need two plastic buckets with handles that you can store easily under your sink. (Remember that the area under your bathroom sink should never contain anything dangerous, like cleansers, razors, etc.) After your child is out of her bath, ask her to help you play Pick-up Pals. Explain that in this game, the object is to see which player can fill her bucket full of bath toys and place it in the cupboard first. Play according to your child's speed and capability.

Each time your child completes the game successfully, give her a gold star or sticker. Give your child the message that she is really getting bigger by being so helpful and learning how to clean up.

Guess Which Room
I Am In

Materials

• Your dining room and its contents

Acquaint your toddler with the dining room by using a simple guessing game. Toddlers love such games, and just by participating, they seem to increase their language skills almost by the minute.

Begin by taking a look at your dining room. You can also use your breakfast table or a card table if you prefer not to use the dining room. However, a place in your house in which you and your toddler actually eat will be helpful and help to acquaint your toddler with the sorts of things that are found in this room. Notice the kinds of things that are commonly found in dining rooms, as well as those things that are unique. Some common dining room items might include the following:

• dining table
• dishes
• silverware
• glasses
• centerpiece or flower arrangement

• chairs
• buffet or china cabinet
• salt and pepper shakers
• tablecloths or placemats

Tell your toddler that you are going to say some clues about a special room in your house to see if he can guess what room it is. Go through the process of giving clues until your child correctly guesses the room. Follow up the guessing game by looking in the dining room together and discussing all of the things you gave as clues. Then play the rest of the games in this section.

Plate Color Relay

Materials

- Five to 10 white paper plates per player
- Crayons in assorted colors
- Your dining table

Don't get excited—your toddler and you are not going to dash around breaking expensive dishes in this relay. Instead, you are going to use paper plates for safe and interesting relay fun. This quiet relay asks your child to be quick on his feet, rather than move his feet quickly— and it's easy to prepare.

To begin, all you have to do is cover paper plates with various colors of crayon. Make sets of two of each color. Your toddler will love to help you do this. It isn't important to color each plate neatly or completely, only that each plate has only one color of crayon.

Before playing, use the colored plates as giant color flash cards to practice color recognition. Determine which colors your child knows, then add a few that are a little more difficult to guess.

Now, each player stands on either side of the dining room table, holding the plates upside down so that the colors cannot be seen. Each player takes a turn turning over a plate and identifying its color. If the player does so, he or she places the plate on the table. This goes on until one player has made a line of plates from one end of the table to the other and wins. Try it again, adding more colors as your toddler learns their names. This simple game is a lot of fun and will teach your child the names of colors as well as the concept of taking turns.

Can You Set the Table?

Materials

- Plastic or paper dishes
- Plastic forks and spoons
- Plastic or paper cups
- Placemats
- Paper napkins
- Salt and pepper shakers

Even the youngest toddler is interested in doing what Mommy or Daddy does. In this game, your child will play against himself or another toddler or sibling to duplicate a table setting. Begin this activity by gathering together the table-setting equipment that you will need. Check the materials list for ideas.

Show your child the picture on page 109 and discuss all the items that go into a place setting. Then set a place at the table exactly as you would like your toddler and any other player to set their own places, allowing them to observe. Give the signal to go. The first player to completely copy the example wins.

Try the game again, this time using a timer. Time your toddler and see how long it takes him to copy the place setting. Try another variation of this game and draw a picture of a place setting and see if the players can set their own place setting using the picture. Soon, you will have help setting the table.

Can You Set the Table? *(cont.)*

Ball Roll Game

Materials

- Two cardboard boxes
- One or two cans of tennis balls

Stuck indoors on a rainy day? Maybe you and your toddler need a diversion. This easy-to-do ball game requires very little preparation and means instant fun for the two of you. Begin by finding two cardboard boxes and searching the garage for that old can of tennis balls. Clear off the dining room table and get ready to play. You might want to have a piece of paper for a score card to make the competition more interesting.

At each end of the table, place a cardboard box on the floor. Now, roll the balls slowly across the table and see how many you can each get in the boxes. (Your toddler may need to stand on a chair.) The player with the most balls in the boxes wins.

Vary the game in a number of ways. Get a marking pen and draw happy faces on several of the tennis balls. Give extra points for the number of happy-face balls that each player can get in the box. Or write numbers from 1 to 5 on the balls and give points for each ball in the box at the end of the game. Don't expect your toddler to understand the concept of adding numbers together, but remember that any time you expose your child to number conversation you are setting the stage for later learning in mathematics.

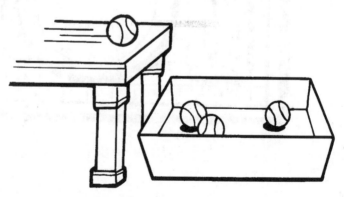

Giant Tic-Tac-Toe

Materials

- Construction paper
- Large felt-tipped marker
- Clear shelf paper
- Scissors
- Shirt box for storage

Who knows why even the tiniest child loves this old standard—but they do. Make a set of ten 5" x 5" (13 cm x 13 cm) cards out of construction paper, marking half with X and half with O; your toddler can help you with this. You can laminate the cards with clear shelf paper if you'd like. Then, make a giant tic-tac-toe board on butcher paper, with 6" x 6" (15 cm x 15 cm) spaces so that the cards can be easily placed.

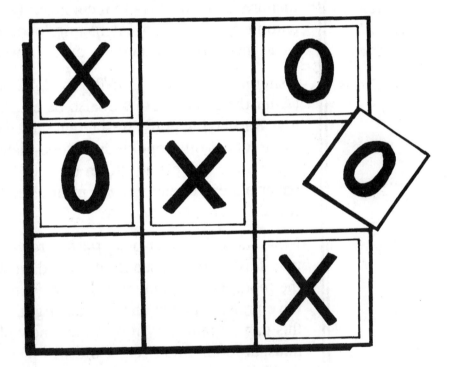

Now you and your toddler are ready to play. Place the game board on the dining room table so that you will have a lot of playing space. Vary the game by using a score card to keep track of who has won more games. Use a shirt box to store your game when you have finished playing.

Food Flash Cards

Materials

- Thin, inexpensive paper plates
- Old magazines
- Newspaper food section or supermarket circulars
- Nontoxic glue or paste
- Safety scissors

This game is a load of fun, and the preparation is just as enjoyable as the game itself. Toddlers are usually more fascinated with toy food than they are with eating the real thing, so you might as well take advantage of this fact and capture their attention.

For this game you will need a package of inexpensive, thin paper plates; old magazines or the newspaper food section; and glue. The best kinds of pictures are those that are large and easy to recognize. Devote some time to cutting out pictures of interesting food. (You might want to do this part of the activity over a few weeks.)

Using nontoxic glue, glue the food pictures to the plates. (After the game, these will also be excellent hands-on toys for playing house, restaurant, and so on.) Be sure to make lots of different kinds of food plates to make the game more interesting. After the glue is dry, turn the paper plate over and in large print write the name of the food.

Now, stack the paper-plate flash cards and begin. Hold up a flash card and see if your child tell you the name of the food. Do it again until she can identify them all. Give praise for each one she gets right. When you play this game again, vary it by adding new plates with more unusual food. Soon your child will increase her food vocabulary dramatically.

Another variation is to draw pictures of food on the paper plates. This is an excellent variation to keep your toddler busy. Just remember that many toddlers will not be able to draw pictures that you or she will be able to identify, but the practice is an excellent way to build fine motor skills.

Paper Hamburger Sequencing Game

Materials

- Construction paper in a variety of colors
- Scissors
- Clear shelf paper
- Storage box

Hamburgers are such a big part of the food scene that it isn't long before a toddler knows exactly what one is. In this game, you make a pretend meal, as well as teach important sequencing skills that are part of his or her cognitive development.

Begin by purchasing a multi-color package of construction paper and some clear shelf paper. Don't worry, you don't have to be an artist to make this game. Now outline and cut out the following paper hamburger ingredients, being sure to make a set for each player:

- two round shapes for pieces of a bun
- one round, meat patty
- one square for cheese
- a smaller, round shape for ketchup
- small, green shapes for pickles
- a round shape for onion
- a free-form shape for a lettuce leaf

Pick paper colors that most closely match the real thing. Make the shapes look more realistic by adding a few details with a black felt pen. Use clear shelf paper to cover the pieces so that your new game will hold up under toddler wear-and-tear.

Now, you are ready to play. Place the pieces of hamburger at one end of the dining room on a plate. Give oral directions for the players to go to the plate for a certain piece of the hamburger. Players must walk over, get the piece, walk back, and add it to their hamburger. Each player has to put his or her hamburger together in a way that makes sense. The first one with a finished hamburger wins.

Toddler Magicians

Materials

- Three plastic cups
- A toy or small ball
- Library book of magic tricks (optional)

Very young children are often fascinated with magic tricks. Some even dream of becoming magicians. This simple game requires practically no preparation and allows a toddler to perfect her slight-of-hand.

Begin by getting three plastic or paper cups. Next, find a small object like a ball or a small toy that will easily fit under a cup. Have your child be the magician and hide the object under a cup.

Show her how to move the cups around to confuse her audience, and then see who can guess where the object is. You can play this game again and again and give everyone turns.

You can check out books at the library with simple tricks and encourage your toddler and siblings or pals to come up with a magic show.

Face Puzzles

Materials

- Thin, inexpensive, white paper plates
- Crayons
- Scissors
- Resealable plastic bags

If you have an hour or two, you can make this interesting game that your child will use again and again. These simple face puzzles can help your toddler begin to identify facial expressions and feelings.

Begin by making the puzzles. One way to prepare these simple puzzles is to get your older child involved. A six-year-old is often quite able to help you prepare these simple puzzles and will enjoy making a game for a younger sibling. Just draw a very simple face on paper plate, giving each a different expression: happy, sad, angry, and so forth. The simpler, the better for a toddler to be able to visualize how the face should look when the pieces are put together. Now, cut the plate into two, three, or four pieces to make a little puzzle.

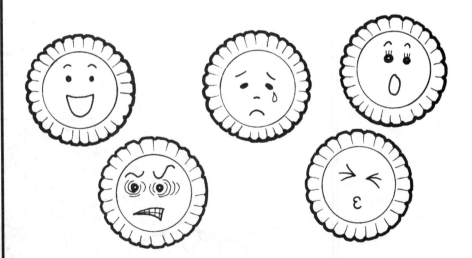

Let your toddler play the puzzle game again and again. Give a prize or a hug for each puzzle correctly assembled. (Don't forget to slip a few of these into your purse or backpack for road trips.)

Breakfast, Lunch, and Dinner Grouping Game

Materials

- Food flash cards (see page 112)

In order to play this game, you will need food flash cards (see page 112 for instructions). If you have already prepared food flash cards, take a look at them to make sure you have a wide variety of foods, especially those that can be categorized as breakfast, lunch, and dinner foods. Here are some suggestions for each meal category:

Breakfast Foods

- cereal in bowls or boxes
- bacon and eggs
- muffins
- orange juice or other fruit juices
- milk or chocolate milk
- toast
- pancakes

Breakfast, Lunch, and Dinner Grouping Game *(cont.)*

Materials

- Food flash cards (see page 112)

Lunch Foods

- hamburgers
- hot dogs
- PB&J sandwiches (peanut butter and jelly)
- French fries
- potato chips
- carrot and celery sticks

Dinner Foods

- fried or baked chicken
- casseroles
- meat loaf and potatoes
- spaghetti or pizza
- tacos, rice and beans
- sushi

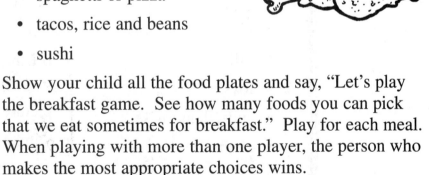

Show your child all the food plates and say, "Let's play the breakfast game. See how many foods you can pick that we eat sometimes for breakfast." Play for each meal. When playing with more than one player, the person who makes the most appropriate choices wins.

Note: Many family-style restaurants and coffee shops have paper children's menus with photographs of plates of food. These free menus make a wonderful source for pictures of various meals.

Guess Which Room
I Am In

Materials

• Your bedroom and its contents

Acquaint your toddler with the room in which you play all of the games in this section by a simple guessing game. Toddlers love guessing games, and when they participate in trying to guess, they are increasing their language skills by the minute!

Begin by taking a look at the bedroom you will play these games in. (It doesn't matter if you choose to use your own bedroom or your toddler's for these games; in fact, you may want to vary it for fun. Think about all of the things you commonly find in a bedroom. Use this list to jog your memory, and go take a look at the bedroom before you begin to mention things to your toddler that are specific for his or her own bedroom.

- bed
- chest of drawers
- closet
- clothes
- pillow
- toys
- stuffed animals
- chair

- blankets
- sheets
- bedspread
- mirror
- brushes, combs, and other grooming items
- pictures, photographs
- window

Now, investigate the bedroom with your toddler. Begin by asking him to play a guessing game. Mention the common things he will find in the bedroom and see if he can guess. Keep giving him clues until he guesses, and then follow up by looking for each item you talked about. Afterwards, play the rest of the games in this section.

Stuffed Animal Hamper Toss

Materials

- Two laundry baskets
- Stuffed animals

Most toddlers have lots and lots of stuffed animals. They make wonderful toys for toddlers because they are soft and have no edges.

For this game, you will need your toddler's stuffed animal collection and two laundry hampers. (You can use any suitable large container, of course.) Count out an even number of stuffed animals for each player. The size of the stuffed animal doesn't matter. They can be tiny or gigantic—the more you vary the size, the more amusing the game will be to you and your toddler. Place the hampers several feet away from the throw line.

Each player takes a turn at throwing a stuffed animal until they are all gone. See how many each player was able to throw into his or her basket. Then play again. The player with the most animals in the basket wins. There are many different variations for this game. Try counting as you go along with the game to teach basic number skills, or move the basket further away after each throw. You might even try it blindfolded.

Guess What I Am Taking on Vacation

Materials

- Items from your bedrooms
- An old suitcase or backpack for each player

You don't have to leave your house to have the fun of going on vacation with your toddler. All you need is a suitcase or backpack for each of you, and simple items you find in both your rooms. This imaginative guessing game can keep your toddler entertained practically any time.

Begin this game by talking about packing for vacation. Talk about vacation experiences you have had in the past with your toddler. You might say, for example, "Remember when we went to Grandma's? Let's see if we can remember what we packed. We packed clothes like pants, dresses, socks and shoes, and we brought our bathing suits so we could go swimming." And so on.

Now, get ready to play. Each player picks a pretend place he or she is going and then packs. The other player tries to guess what each player has packed in his or her suitcase. As each player guesses, the other player checks, and if he or she has indeed packed that item, the item is taken out and put in a pile. Alternate turns—and no peeking. The first person to guess everything in the other player's suitcase wins.

Vary this game to make it easier or more difficult for your toddler by choosing the number of items you both pack. You can even start with one item. You can also alter this game again and again by deciding ahead of time what pretend "vacation" you are going on. For example, you would pack different things to go to the beach than you would to go to the mountains.

Sleeping Santa Game

Materials

- A pillowcase
- Some of your toddler's toys

Toddlers who celebrate the Christmas holiday are enchanted with Santa. Here is a game you can play with your toddler to make it easier to take an afternoon nap when the excitement of the season is upon you.

Practice the game by getting an empty pillowcase and telling your child that you are going to take turns pretending to be Santa. The idea of the game is to take turns filling the sack with several toys from your toddler's room. Then one player pretends to be Santa and delivers the toys while the other player pretends to be asleep waiting for Santa to come. When the "gifts" arrive, the napper can awaken and pretend to be delighted.

To get your toddler to sleep, tell her that if she closes her eyes and goes right to sleep, while she is sleeping you will pretend to be Santa and deliver gifts just like you have played before.

Make this activity more fun by occasionally supplying a new toy. The object of the game is that your toddler must actually go to sleep—and no peeking. The moment she is asleep, arrange the pretend delivery where she will see it. Don't wait until the last minute to do this or you may lose the moment and lose credibility with your toddler.

You may find that your toddler begins to ask to take an afternoon nap once she associates it with a pleasant surprise.

Goodnight, Goodnight

Materials

• A copy of *Goodnight Moon*

When your toddler is all wound up and can't seem to get herself to sleep, it's time to pull out your top reinforcement—your well-worn copy of *Goodnight Moon* by Margaret Wise Brown (HarperCollins Children's Books, 1947, 1975). Tell your toddler that you're going to play a quiet game that will help her go to sleep. Snuggle up on her bed and read *Goodnight Moon* as slowly as you can. If your toddler hasn't settled down with one reading, read it again even more slowly. Then invite your toddler to slide under the covers and slowly say goodnight to the items around her in her room. If she speeds up, gently remind her to go slowly. If she's not yet drowsy, go around the room again. By this time, she should be quite tired and you can say goodnight to each other as you tiptoe away. This is also a good way to get your toddler calmed down when you are sleeping in a place away from home so that she becomes comfortable with her surroundings.

What's Missing?

Materials

- Your bed
- Several safe objects from your room or your toddler's room

This game is lots of fun and even the smallest toddler can begin to learn to play it. One nice thing about this game is that you can easily increase the level of difficulty to challenge your toddler as his skill level changes.

For this game, you will need several small objects from your dresser or your child's dresser. Pick small objects that are not dangerous. Now place these objects on the bed in a group. Start this game with two items, then add three and so on, depending on the age and skill level of 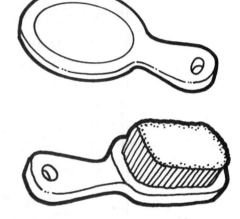 your toddler. Ask your toddler to look carefully at what is on the bedspread. Name the items with your toddler, and make sure he can name the items, too. Now, ask your toddler to close his eyes as you take one of the items away. Ask him which item is missing. Then try again, varying the game by taking more items away each time, and possibly adding more as well.

Now, try it again, this time with you as the player. Sometimes you will actually find in games of this nature that your toddler quickly becomes more of an expert than you, possibly because he has few pressing demands to distract him. Practice this game again and again with your toddler—give the winner kisses or a sticker. Over time, this game will improve memory, concentration, and cognitive thinking skills.

Pirate's Hidden Treasure

Materials

- Art supplies
- Found items
- Small box

In this game you and your toddler will be pirates finding hidden treasures. Creative play is one of the most important kinds of play your toddler does. Through creative play your child discovers the world and who he is, as well as increases his imagination, empathy, and understanding.

Find a small cardboard box about the size of a small jewelry box. In fact, if you have a small, unused box that once held earrings, a bracelet, or a ring, this will make a wonderful treasure chest. Spend some time with your toddler preparing for the game by making or finding treasure. You can do this with simple art supplies or discover things that make excellent treasure in your junk drawer.

Here are some ideas for treasures that you and your toddler can find or easily make at home:

- paper coins cut from paper and decorated
- a treasure map you both work on together with art supplies
- old costume jewelry
- old plastic jewelry covered with white, nontoxic glue and glitter
- used, brightly-colored, foil wrapping paper

After you and your toddler finish preparing or finding your treasures, help your toddler to place the items in the treasure box you have chosen. Each player takes turns hiding the treasure somewhere in the bedroom and the other player searches for it. The pirate who hides the treasure can give clues or hints or say, "cold, warm, or hot," depending upon how close the searching pirate is to discovering the box. Most toddlers will enjoy playing this again and again.

Sock Toss

Materials

- Clean socks
- Your sock drawer

Have you ever wished that keeping your house orderly was more fun? This game helps you and your toddler to make some otherwise tedious chores more enjoyable. It is a perfect game for laundry day.

Begin by washing your socks. Let your toddler help with this process—finding all the socks, washing and drying them, and finally matching and sorting the clean socks.

To play, you will need to roll pairs of socks into toss-able balls. In case you don't normally roll socks, just place the socks on top of one another, turn down the edge of one sock so that it rolls over the other sock and stuff the socks in as you roll.

Toss your rolled socks right into the drawer to earn points. Take turns tossing; the player who gets the most socks in the drawer wins. If you don't want to toss socks into the drawer, use a laundry basket or a cardboard box for a target. Vary the game by moving further back and throwing or giving small stickers for each sock that you throw that lands inside the drawer.

Doll Hide and Seek

Materials

- One or more of your toddler's dollies
- You and your toddler's imaginations

Most toddlers love baby dolls. Perhaps it is because dolls are in a sense a reflection of their most important relationships—that of their parents and themselves. This is an excellent reason to make your toddler's dollies part of the fun. Dolls are also an excellent way for toddlers to model appropriate social behavior, especially those without siblings—and boys can be encouraged to play with them, too.

Ask your toddler to pick a dolly to play with the two of you. This dolly is going to be hidden in a game of hide-and-seek. You and your toddler take turns hiding the dolly and seeking it out. Keep track of how many times each player can find the dolly to see who is the winner. Set some rules about where each player can hide the doll, and try it with a variety of dolls of different shapes and sizes.

This is also an excellent game to inspire dramatic play and role-playing. Encourage your child to give her dolly a character, like a puppet, and make her dolly talk. And you give it a try—remember that creative play is always more fun if everyone uses his imagination and gets involved. Some parents hesitate to play imaginary games with their children, fearful that their children won't grasp reality, but researchers have proven that dramatic play and role-playing is a healthy part of early childhood development. So don't worry, just enjoy.

Little Big Lists

- Objects found in your or your child's bedroom
- Pen or pencil
- Notebook

This is a fun and easy game that you and your toddler can play in your bedroom or anywhere at all. This game will help you teach your toddler the meaning behind the words "big" and "little." Before beginning this interesting and simple game, talk with your child in casual conversation for a few days, using the words "big" and "little" to describe the things you both do and see. You might talk about your surroundings, saying, "Isn't that a big dog? It's much bigger than grandma's dog." Or, "I only want a little piece of pie, very little, like this." As you do this, your child will begin to understand not only the meanings of the words but the differences in sizes and how objects compare in size.

Using a large sheet of paper or a notebook, label one page with the word "big" and another with the word "little." Ask your child to help you play the game of locating and naming things in the room that are either big or little. As you find them, write them down on the list. The winner is the person that can find the most items in each category.

Little
pencil
penny

Big
couch
chair
pillow

Vary the game by deciding who will look for big objects and who will look for little objects, or see who can name two big objects first and so on. Soon your child will have added the understanding of different sizes and their relationships to one another to his cognitive development.

Guess What My Face Means

Materials

- Large mirror
- You and your toddler

Being able to understand and express emotion appropriately is something that adults strive to do, not just children. Helping your toddler recognize the meaning of facial expressions can help him with social and emotional development.

Most bedrooms contain a mirror. If you don't have a mirror in your bedroom, play this game in a spot in your house that has a mirror large enough for the two of you to look in at the same time. Say to your toddler, "I am going to make a face. Can you tell me what this face means?" Then make a face that shows an emotion. Here are some facial expressions that a toddler should begin to be able to understand:

- happy
- sad
- angry
- surprise
- boredom

- disappointment
- confusion
- worry
- pleasure

Guess What My Face Means *(cont.)*

Materials

- Large mirror
- You and your toddler

Now, as you make each face, see if your child can identify the emotions you are trying to express. Try it again and let your toddler get her chance to make faces. See how many you can identify. Pick a number of faces to try. The player who correctly identifies the greatest number of faces wins. Vary the game by adding different and more subtle emotions as your child gets older and more experienced at the game.

Name the Time Game

Materials

- Scrapbook
- Glue or paste
- Pictures from magazines or drawings

The ability to understand the concept of time is complicated so don't be surprised if your toddler doesn't have very much of an idea about what the time of day is or when certain events take place over the course of a day. However, this simple game can begin to give your child an opportunity to associate concepts with the time of day, an important part of her cognitive development.

Begin this game by creating a book. Find or draw pictures associated with the time of day. Paste or glue these into the scrapbook, one picture to a page so the book doesn't become confusing. After you have a number of pictures, you are ready to play with your toddler.

Sit with your toddler and look at the book. Ask your toddler, "When do we do this activity—morning, afternoon, or nighttime?" Give your child the answer and talk about it until she begins to learn the answer herself. Each time she wins, praise her verbally or give her a sticker. See if she can correctly identify the times of day for all of the pictures. Place this picture book in your regular library and review it occasionally with your child.

Life-Size Puzzles

Materials

- Poster board
- Scissors
- Large-tipped, black felt marker

This interesting game will help a toddler identify the parts of her own body, while having a lot of fun in the process. With a little preparation, you will have a game that your toddler can use again and again.

Get a large roll of butcher paper or other paper large enough to trace your toddler's shape. You can do this with poster board as well; although it is more expensive, it will hold up through more play sessions. Put the paper or poster board on the floor and ask your toddler to lie down on it so you can trace her. Do so using a felt pen with a thick tip. After your toddler gets up, show her what you have done and talk about and label the different parts of her body. Make sure to include and discuss the following:

- face
- arms
- hands
- chest
- legs
- feet

- hair
- eyes, nose, mouth
- fingers
- tummy
- knees
- toes

As you talk about the part of the body, draw enough detail on the section so your toddler can identify it. Then get out the scissors and make a life-size puzzle for your toddler. Cut the puzzle in six pieces so your toddler can easily put it back together: head, arms, hands, torso, legs, feet. Give a reward when he successfully puts it together and another for naming the parts of the body.

This Is Me Puzzle

Materials

- Old photos of your child
- Resealable plastic bags for storage.

For this game, you make a jigsaw puzzle of your child's photo and photos that relate to him directly. Please be sure to cut up copies of your photos or to use photos that won't be missed.

Begin this game by sorting through your extra photos. You might want to do this with your toddler, talking over the photos you choose. Select a few that are of your toddler and that won't be missed by making them part of the game.

Cut the photos into large, easy-to-assemble pieces. Toddlers can't put together a large puzzle or visualize spatial relationships, except for those that are very simple, so be sure this game is something he can accomplish with minimum frustration. Say, "This is a puzzle of you. When you finish it, you will see a picture of yourself." Lay out the puzzle pieces in front of your toddler and have him put them together. Let your toddler try it, and give a hug for every successful attempt.

Cookie Dough Kid

Materials

- You and your toddler

This game requires no preparation, only you, your toddler, and a healthy dose of cuddles and fun. The object of this game is to pretend to make your toddler into a cookie and decorate and bake her in an imaginary oven. Toddlers love this. In fact, parents who have tried this one say that their first-graders still beg to be made into a cookie.

Begin this simple game by asking your toddler if she would like to be made into a cookie. Then, ask your toddler to stretch out. Say, "First, I am going to knead the cookie dough." Give your child a gentle massage. Then say, "Now I am going to cut the cookie dough like a gingerbread boy." Trace around your child with your finger. "Now I am going to decorate the cookie dough." Pretend to add decorations to your "cookie" and watch the giggles start. Then "pop" your child in the oven by rolling him over.

You can play this game again and again, and children will never tire of it. Additionally, this game will make your child feel loved, and it will even help end tears or a bad mood.

Whose Is This?

Materials

- Items from each family member
- Basket or box

When you look at belongings scattered around the room, your brain sorts through information so quickly that you don't even realize all the deductive thinking that goes into figuring out what belongs to whom. No wonder it is sometimes easy to forget that toddlers need to be taught to think in this way.

In this game, you only need things you already have around the house. Collect several items from each family member that easily identify her. Place these in a big box or laundry basket. Ask your toddler to see if she can answer the question, "Whose is this?" Keep going until she can name all the owners. Don't forget to put some of her own belongings into the basket to let her identify which are hers, too.

Vary the game by choosing more objects or less common objects. End the game by putting everyone's objects away. *Note:* This is an excellent game to play when you are trying to clean up. You might even find yourself enjoying clean-up time, too.

Texture Bags

Materials

- Brown bags or plastic containers
- Textured items from around your house

Toddlers love putting their hands on things. The goal of parents is to make sure that what they do get their hands on is safe. This game gives toddlers an excellent opportunity to explore their sense of touch in just such a manner.

First, get some brown paper bags to hold objects that have texture. Another excellent container is a plastic container with a snap-open lid. Then begin to explore your house to see what kinds of textures you can find to put in the bags. Use the list below to give you some ideas:

- sand
- rocks
- flour
- rice
- brush
- fabric

- fruit
- large beads
- pasta
- small toys
- sponges
- string

These are just a few ideas to get you started making texture bags from things found around your house. Explore your own surroundings with your hands to discover many more. (Make sure the items are not dangerous before adding them to a texture bag.)

Now try the game with your toddler. Ask your toddler to put his hand inside the bag and try to tell you what he feels without looking. Try again until he guesses correctly. Vary the game by adding more objects.

Voice Memory Tapes

Materials

- Blank cassette tape
- Tape recorder with microphone
- Willing family members

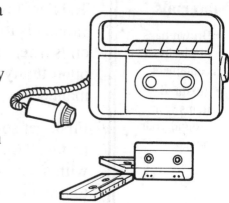

One of the first signs that a very young child's mental and emotional processes are developing is his ability to distinguish between himself and other people. This sense of self begins in infancy and normally develops through young adulthood.

This game will help your child identify the voice of those people around him. It is also a very interesting way to make a usable and preservable time capsule for your child. You will need a blank tape and a tape recorder with a microphone. Ask family members and others who are close to your toddler to participate, making a recording of their voices with a happy message or maybe a song. Consider using the script below for those family members who are a little microphone-shy. Remind everyone that this isn't supposed to be a masterpiece, just a lovely little game and keepsake for your child.

Script Idea:

Hello there! Can you guess who this is? I love you very much, and your mommy (or daddy) has asked me to sing a little song for you on this tape. While I sing, see if you can guess who I am! Here goes. (Sing a short song, like "Row, Row, Row Your Boat," or other song that the toddler thinks is special.)

Now, play the finished tape for your child. See if he can guess to whose voice he is listening. Even after he has guessed all the people's voices, he will still love hearing family and friends sing to him again and again.

Clown Faces

Materials

- Clown makeup kit
- Clown clothes
- Clean-up supplies

Bored? This game will entertain your child all afternoon and be a lasting memory of something special you did together.

Before beginning this game, you will need to make a trip to the costume store or any department store that sells stage makeup. Also, around Halloween, many stores will carry simple stage make-up. Select the following for your clown make-up kit:

- white clown makeup
- black greasepaint sticks
- red greasepaint sticks
- face powder and a brush
- cold cream for makeup removal
- tissues and paper towels

And consider some of the following:

- red clown noses
- wigs
- funny hats

Make sure to check your closets and your own costume supplies to see what you have on hand before you begin. Now, you and your toddler can get into some old clothes and you are ready to begin. Start by applying clown white all over your faces. Your toddler can help with this. Now ask your toddler to let you help her with the hard parts. Use the simple clown diagram above for some ideas, or just make up your own. After you have both completed your clown makeup, find some funny clothes and get the other members of your family involved judging your makeup and tricks to see who wins. This is also an excellent idea for siblings and small groups of toddlers to try.

Nesting Boxes Game

Materials

- Boxes and lids of different sizes
- Art materials

Maybe you have a nesting dolls set, one in which a large doll holds a smaller doll with a still smaller doll inside and so on. This game borrows from the idea of this traditional doll, but it is something you can make in a few minutes and use with your toddler for hours of fun.

First, find some old boxes with lids of various sizes. These should be easy-to-open boxes. Pick up different-sized boxes from a discount or craft store, or save them after holiday celebrations. Try the lids and make sure they go on and off easily so that your toddler won't be frustrated. Decorate the boxes with markers, wrapping paper, or glitter before you stack them to make them more interesting to your toddler.

Show your toddler the decorated boxes and let her pull the nests apart and put them back together. She wins if she can do it. Advance the game by timing her or letting her time herself with an egg timer. You can also make a separate game for another player and have players compete against each other. Use the words "big," "bigger," "biggest," and so forth to help your child identify the sizes of the boxes and increase vocabulary.

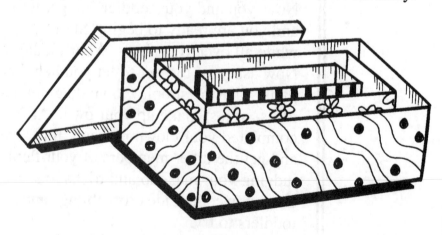

Quiet as a Mouse

Materials

- Small pillow or beanbag

Shhh! Do you hear that sound? It's silence. And it is something that parents of toddlers hear very little. This activity will help you teach your toddler that being quiet can be a game.

Begin this game by teaching your child this simple poem:

Quiet Little Mouse

I am very quiet,
I am quiet as a mouse.
You can hardly even hear me
As I move around the house.

And as I walk on tippy toes,
You'll have to look to see
That this quiet little mouse
Is really me!

Then ask your child to practice walking like a mouse. Tiptoe together in a room, making sure to whisper quietly or not talk at all. You may find that you need to practice this again and again with your toddler.

Now play the game. One player sits in the room with her eyes closed and places a small pillow in front of her, which is the "cheese." Then the "mouse" sneaks in. If the player hears the mouse, she opens her eyes and says, "I got you, little mouse!" If the player doesn't hear the mouse, the mouse must grab the cheese and tiptoe away. The mouse wins if she get the cheese before the other player knows it is gone.

Color Hunt

Materials

- Lightweight basket with handle
- Colored construction paper
- Scissors
- Felt-tip pen
- Various objects around the house

This simple game is a takeoff of an Easter egg hunt, but this time around, you and your toddler are hunting for colors. Begin by gathering materials. You will need a couple of lightweight baskets with handles. Cut out circles of various colors of construction paper and, with a felt pen, clearly label them with the appropriate color.

Before playing the game, test your toddler about his color-recognition skills. Hold up a circle and ask him if he knows the name of the color. When he guesses correctly, say, "That is right, and here is the word that spells red." After your child can recognize a few of the colors, you are ready to play the game.

Take a color circle and place it in the bottom of a basket. This becomes the color your toddler will hunt for. Ask him to go in his room, or any other room you choose, and put things in the basket that are the same color as the circle. Give him a sticker or prize for each item he selects correctly.

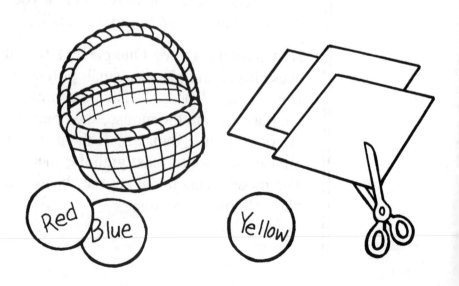

Stepping Stone Game

Materials

- Poster board
- Laminating paper
- Scissors
- Adhesive Velcro strips

If you're like most parents of toddlers, you are anxious to figure out a way to get them to go where you want. Toddlers are notorious for running around (and away) with their high level of exuberance. Use this game as a model for following you in an enjoyable way.

This game requires a few materials and some simple preparation that you can easily do, perhaps while you are watching your favorite program. You will need sheets of poster board in several colors, clear shelf paper, and scissors or an artist's knife. (An artist's knife should be kept stored away from children.)

Cut out square "stepping stones" from the poster board. These should be in a variety of colors and around one square foot in size. Then laminate each square with clear shelf paper so that it will last through normal wear-and-tear. Attach Velcro strips to the bottom of each stepping stone to prevent slipping on the carpet. If you are going to use the stepping stones on a hardwood or linoleum surface, masking tape will secure them so that they do not slip.

Explain to your toddler that you are both going to use your make-believe skills to pretend you are going across an imaginary lake, river, or pool. Then show your toddler the stepping stones and explain that the object of the game is to walk on them. Now play follow-the-leader across the pretend water. Vary the game by changing the path of the stones, letting your child be the leader and so on. The winner is the person who can make it to the other side of the imaginary river without stepping off the stones.

Felt Board and Fall Leaves

Materials

- Purchased felt board or large piece of felt covering a board
- Felt pieces
- Scissors

If you are feeling a little bit creative and have a few hours on your hands, there are a number of easy toddler games that you can construct yourself and save a lot of money at the same time. One of the things that many parents with toddlers are constantly faced with is the pressure to buy more toys for their children. The next few games in this section will give the information you need to make some low cost, interesting games.

Begin by visiting your craft store. You are going to construct a low-cost, easy-to-make felt board that you can use in this game and in several others in this book. Felt boards are a valuable addition to your child's educational play. A felt board can be as simple as a large piece of felt tacked to an old bulletin board, or you can buy an inexpensive one at a school supply or craft store. Then just cut a variety of large, simple leaves in a variety of fall colors, and you are ready.

The object of the game is to see which player can place all of his fall leaves on the tree first. Begin by dividing the leaves equally between two players and saying, "Go!" Now, you and your toddler press on your felt, autumn leaves. See who wins. Then, play again with your eyes closed or using only one hand. Most toddlers will be content to do this the simple way. However, variations are nice when you are playing with an older sibling.

Face Race

Materials

- Felt board
- Felt scraps

Toddlers love faces. This game gives your child another opportunity to be fascinated with faces and create his own, too, using a felt board and felt (see page 144 for another idea using felt). All you need are scraps of felt left over from any other craft project. Just cut eyes, noses, mouths, hair, hats, and anything else your toddler associates with a face. Now, show him how to make a face out of the pieces on the felt board. Let him practice until he is ready to race, and then see who can make a face the fastest! You will both have lots of fun.

Vary this game by adding more toddlers or more playing pieces, or, if your toddler is playing alone, have him make more than one face to win. Make sure to talk about the names for the parts of the face as you go along, and you will increase his vocabulary, too.

Balloon Golf

Materials

- Balloons
- Plastic bucket
- Plastic golf club or plastic bat

Toddlers love to hit things. They love to hear the noises and see what will happen. They are interested in the experiment itself and in your reaction. Here is a game that will give you an opportunity to tell your toddler to hit something and have it be perfectly fine with you. This game also will increase his eye-hand coordination and large motor skills.

This golf game requires several balloons, a child-size, plastic golf club or bat and a bucket. Balance an inflated balloon on the bucket and give your child the golf club. His goal is to swing and hit the balloon, making it fly in the air. This is harder than it seems for a toddler, and he will love to do it.

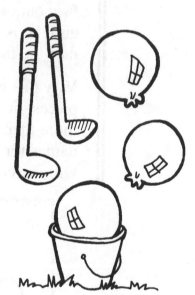

This game can have variations. Have a number of balloons for your child to hit and ask him to name the colors or balloons he is hitting. See who can hit the balloon the farthest, or let him take turns with an older sibling.

What Goes Together?

Materials

- Pairs of items found around the house

What goes together? Pairs of things! Why does it seem like on any given day, you can't find the mate of anything in your house? Shoes, socks, you name it, the matching pairs are nowhere to be found. This game will help you get organized and give your toddler time to learn about pairs. It can even be done as part of your normal housecleaning time and become a game you share together often.

To play the game, find pairs of things in the house. Here are some suggestions:

- shoes
- socks
- gloves
- mittens
- salt and pepper shakers
- bookends

Play the game as you go about your cleaning. Hold up one of a pair and say, "Help me find the other one that looks just like this and then it will become a pair!" Play until you find everything.

If you happened to be ultra-organized and nary a pair of shoes ever gets mislaid at your house, you can take out shoes and socks and scramble them in a pile on the floor. Let your toddler match the pairs together.

Chicken and the Egg Game

Materials

- Paper plates
- Scissors
- Crayons
- Magazines or old coloring books

An early preschool skill is to be able to sort items into categories and to decide what does and what does not belong in a group. This little game will take you about a half an hour to prepare, uses materials from right around the house, and will give your child practice at this important skill.

To prepare, draw some chicks on white, inexpensive paper plates. You do not have to be an artist to do this, just draw a large yellow ball with beak and eyes—your child will understand the picture. Now draw several other objects on paper plates. These objects should be totally unrelated to the chicks. A shoe, a hat, a clock, a window, a girl, a boy, or a dog are just some suggestions of unrelated objects that are easy to draw. If you feel uncomfortable drawing, cut pictures of objects from an old coloring book or a magazine.

Line the "eggs" up on the table and place the two chicks and one other object drawing under three of them. Now let your toddler explore and tell you what doesn't belong. Play again and again until your child is an expert. Give a reward or praise to keep it interesting.

Dolly's Bedtime Race

Materials

- Your toddler's dollies
- A towel or washcloth "blankie" for each doll

Have you ever wondered why your toddler hates the one thing tired parents wait for all day? This ritual game will make the race into a bed enjoyable although it can be played at other times. All you need are some small, clean cloths and several dolls from your toddler's collection.

Set up the dollies in a row on the floor. These are the dollies that your toddler must put to bed. In order to put one to bed, your toddler must kiss the doll, place it on the floor, and cover it carefully with a small cloth.

Once your toddler understands, say, "Go!" and let the fun begin. This is also a wonderful party game or a game for two or more toddlers. This game will inspire creative play as well as give your child an opportunity to practice following directions. Play until your toddler is tired.

Pillow Games

Materials

- Pillows
- Play area

Pillows make wonderful toys. If your toddler trips, she has a toddler safety net. If she wants to take a little rest, she is all ready. Here are a few quick suggestions for toddler relay races using pillows.

Game 1: Toddler Baby Crawl

For this game you will need all the pillows you can find in the house. Line them up, end-to-end, in a row across the living room or other large area in your house. The object of this game is to crawl across the pillows and back. It's that simple. Line up two toddlers and a row of pillows for each and say, "Go!" The winner gets a hug. Try again.

Game 2: Grab-a-Pillow Running Race

For this game, stack the pillows at the end of the playing area. Each toddler runs to the pillow stack, grabs a pillow, and runs back carrying it in front of her. If she falls, she will land softly. This game is a lot of fun for everyone and ends up looking very silly.

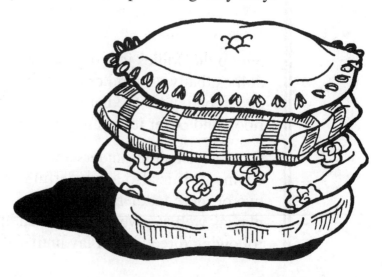

Treasure Hunt Hug Game

Materials

- Love
- Hugs
- Red hearts
- Heart container

This game has one purpose—to make your day with your toddler more loving. It often seems parents are so busy they forget to give affection. As children grow older they want fewer hugs—so it's important to give hugs while children are little and need to be touched to feel loved. This game is designed to help you celebrate the perfect, miraculous relationship you share with your toddler. Use it to remind yourself how much you have to be thankful for every day.

Begin by cutting some hearts out of red paper. Explain to your child that whenever he sees a heart trail in the house he should follow it. Place the heart trail on the floor and wait with open arms at the other end. If he doesn't notice, draw some attention to the trail and let the hugs begin. Make sure you are always there at the other end. Don't get the phone or answer the door—they can wait, but your child should not.

Place your paper hearts in a special container and let your child use them to give you or other family members a hug, too, or organize impromptu group hugs. This game will end up being your very favorite. Warmest wishes to you and your toddler!

Outing Survival Kit

Traveling with your toddler, whether it is down the street or across the country, can be a challenge. Having a survival kit isn't just a cute idea; it's a necessity. Save your sanity with these super survival kit ideas.

- Don't throw that old baby bag away; you can still use it to cart around your survival equipment for you and your toddler.

- Buy small containers of baby wipes. These work well in a bag, and there are a million times a day you will wish you could clean up your toddler, your own fingers, or something else that is too sticky to stand!

- Toddlers are often in need of a little bit of first aid. Keep adhesive bandages and antiseptic on hand to allow you to take care of boo-boos before they get uncomfortable.

- Juice boxes are imperative for your sanity and your toddler's good humor. A box of juice after a long play session can improve the mood of any tired toddler.

- Give your child something cuddly—a favorite toy or blanket—to cozy up with during those long rides home.

- Keep handy a coin purse with coins. It's amazing how many toddlers love those little rides you see outside of stores. And for 25 cents, you can indulge your toddler and keep your budget, too!

- You never know when you will need identification or your emergency phone numbers. There is nothing worse then having car problems and not being able to remember your husband's co-worker's extension.

- Carry little snacks with you. Try some of the dried fruit snacks that look so much like candy your toddler will never know. A plastic container of cereal can save the day, too.

Toddler Rewards

From very early on, you can give your toddler rewards to give him the kind of cause-effect feedback that tells him that it is better to do a good job than a poor one. While many parents worry that praise and rewards "spoil" a child, this just isn't true. Rewards make toddlers aware that there is a positive consequence for good behavior. It's just that simple.

The most important thing to remember when giving awards is to use times when there is actually some behavior to reward. This makes the relationship between behavior and consequences real. Don't offer rewards as incentives, but give them for performance and you will never have a spoiled kid.

Also, it is important to remember that tiny steps of progress merit rewards. To a toddler, the simplest behavior can be a gigantic effort. Remember that you may have to scale down expectations to fit the reality that a toddler is just beginning to be able to do practically everything.

Toddler Rewards

Use some or all of these rewards for your toddler's participation in toddler game activities

- Hugs
- Kisses
- Verbal praise: "Good job! Way to go! Super!"
- High five, thumbs up, or a special signal
- Stickers
- A special outing
- A gold star
- A happy face picture
- A chance to help with something
- Extra play time
- Stay up an extra 10 minutes
- A ride on a mechanical horse outside a supermarket
- A paper ribbon
- A computer-printed certificate
- A love note
- Choosing what the family will eat for dinner
- Making a treat together—perhaps instant pudding
- Coloring together
- Reading a story or singing together
- A trip to the park
- A nature walk to look at birds or plants
- A small toy
- Choosing the family's breakfast cereal (mix a sweet one with a healthy one or limit your toddler's selection)
- A friend over to visit or visiting a friend
- Choosing where the family will eat lunch when running errands
- Riding on a swing
- A visit to the pet or fish store

Resources and Annotated Bibliography

Videos

There are many times when watching a good video is just the activity for you and your toddler. Watching a carefully chosen video together is a good way to relax and wind down from a busy day. The following list highlights a special video and lists additional videos within well-produced series.

Barney Videos

Barney and Friends Collection, The Lions Group

Many adults—usually those without toddlers—find Barney dull, but he can't be beat for providing wholesome, developmentally appropriate fun for toddlers. Watching a Barney video will never give a toddler a nightmare or an uncomfortable feeling. This aspect alone makes Barney videos a wise choice for any family video library.

Barney's Imagination Island

This Barney episode was originally a television special. In it, Barney and his friends travel to Imagination Island in a floating ship reminiscent of Peter Pan's boat. The friends have many adventures, including an encounter with a crabby, old professor who makes toys that he doesn't allow children to touch. Naturally, everything ends well, and everyone gets home safely. Lots of songs, great sets, too.

Other videos in the Barney series worth watching include *Barney's Adventure Bus* and *Barney's Alphabet Zoo*.

Resources and Annotated Bibliography *(cont.)*

Videos *(cont.)*

Winnie-the-Pooh Videos

Walt Disney Home Video, The Walt Disney Company

Winnie-the-Pooh and all the creatures who inhabit the Hundred Acre Wood are guaranteed to enchant the crankiest toddler. The creatures who come to life in Christopher Robin's imagination will very likely come to life for your toddler, too.

Winnie-the-Pooh

In this video, Pooh's friend Rabbit wants to cancel Valentine's Day. Rabbit, the nervous wreck of the forest, decides that last year's celebration caused too much trouble. There were Valentines all over the place, making the forest very messy. But the other forest friends rebel, and eventually everyone enjoys a happy Valentine's Day. This animated feature will delight even the youngest child.

Another good video in this series is *Grand Adventure: The Search for Christopher Robin.*

Bananas in Pajamas

Polygram Video, a division of Polygram Records and the Australian Broadcasting Company

These videos feature wonderful fruit-shaped pals imported from Australian children's television. Bananas in Pajamas features live video in which actors wearing fruit costumes play the parts of these adorable, easy-to-understand characters. The videos are done in slapstick, and the plots are simple.

Resources and Annotated Bibliography *(cont.)*

Videos *(cont.)*

Bananas in Pajamas, Cuddles Avenue, 1995

In this delightful adventure, those madcap tricksters, the Bananas, plan tricks on the unsuspecting Teddies! Eventually, and with much merriment, the Teddies figure out the fun, and they get together for a party at the end! The video features three other simple situations, cute costumes, and easy-to-follow story lines for toddlers.

Other videos in the series include *Pajama Party* and *Show Business.*

Spot

Everyone loves Spot, and who can help it? He is a delightful, age-appropriate, animated puppy designed to delight the toddler set.

Where's Spot?

In this video, Spot is lost, and everyone must look for him. Based on the storybook by the same name, Spot's dad looks all over for Spot. Of course, he finds him. This is a delightful story, perfect for any toddler.

Resources and Annotated Bibliography *(cont.)*

Books

Touch and Feel Board Book Series
DK Publishing

This series of books will grab your child's imagination. Each book features pages with actual items to feel as well as information about them. Books in the series include:

> *Touch and Feel Home,* 1998.
>
> *Touch and Feel Farm,* 1998.
>
> *Touch and Feel Wild Animals,* 1998.

My Very First Mother Goose Board Book Series
Candlewick Press

This series of four board books is edited by Iona Opie and illustrated by Rosemary Wells. These books feature many of the unusual and sometimes forgotten Mother Goose rhymes. Without a doubt, you will love these witty and amazing illustrations. Books in this series, all published in 1996, include:

> *Humpty Dumpty and Other Rhymes*
>
> *Pussy Cat, Pussy Cat and Other Rhymes*
>
> *Wee Willie Winkie and Other Rhymes*
>
> *Little Boy Blue and Other Rhymes*

Carlstrom, Nancy White Illustrated by Bruce Degan. *Jesse Bear, What Will*

Resources and Annotated Bibliography (cont.)

Books (cont.)

You Wear? Aladdin Paperbacks, Simon and Schuster, 1996.

Together the author and illustrator weave a tale of a little bear, Jesse, who must decide what to wear. However, he doesn't just put on clothes, he puts on the day, too. At the end of the day, Jesse wears hugs and kisses. This is wonderful tale of security for toddlers.

Russell, Bill. *Spider on the Floor,* Crown Publisher, 1997.

This "Raffi: Songs to Read" book features illustrations by True Kelley. In this book, the song "Spider on the Floor" is comically illustrated and interesting to almost any young child. The book includes sheet music.

Carlisle, Bob and Brooke Carlisle. *Butterfly Kisses.* Little Golden Books, 1996.

Butterfly Kisses is a heart-warming book about a father's love for his daughter. In it, he talks about all the reasons he loves her, including butterfly kisses.

Kearns, Kimberly. *Barney and Me at the Circus.* The Lyons Group, 1997.

Everyone loves Barney, and Barney loves the circus. This Barney book will interest your toddler and teach him all about life under the big top. But this book contains a special feature. Insert a picture of your toddler into a slotted page, and his face is incorporated into the illustrations.

I Spy Little Books, Cartwheel Books, Scholastic, Inc., 1998.

These books by Jean Marzollo are based on the "I Spy" books for older children in which they must hunt for objects on a crowded page. These toddler-appropriate books are just challenging enough for the younger set. Your child will also learn the names of objects and be able to identify them, using these delightful little books.

Resources and Annotated Bibliography *(cont.)*

Books *(cont.)*

Ahlberg, Janet and Allan. *Peek-a-Boo!* Puffin Books, 1981.

This book contains several cut-out circles. Through each one, a baby looks into his world. Each illustration is from the baby's perspective as he sees his family going through its daily routine. This particular family lives in England during World War II. The story's clever rhyme and wonderful pictures will delight your toddler who is not so far removed from babyhood.

Brown, Margaret Wise. *The Important Book.* Harper and Row, 1949.

The Important Book tells about all kinds of things that are important and the reason for their importance. Each page includes something else that could be considered important. None of the things talked about are earth-shattering discoveries but rather, the ordinary, everyday kinds of things that we encounter in our lives

Joosee, Barbara. *Mama, Do You Love Me?* Chronicle Books, 1991.

In this book, a little Inuit girl asks her mother the age-old childhood question, "Mama, do you love me?" The little girl begins to question her mother as to how much. The mother replies by using various animals and items from the Inuit culture to reassure her daughter that if ever she became a polar bear and scared her own mother, she should still love her child dearly. This wonderfully comforting book gives the reader a glimpse into the richness of the Inuit culture.

Scarry, Richard. *Richard Scarry's Cars and Trucks and Things That Go.* Western Publishing, 1974.

This book is filled with pictures of every conceivable type of transportation. The Pig Family has a grand adventure as they travel, go to the beach, and see trucks, trains, trolleys, and other things that go.